INDIE AUTHOR MAGAZINE

HELLO AND WELCOME!

I'm Indie Annie, and I'm thrilled you're reading this gorgeous full-color version of IAM. Did you know that you can also access all the information, education, and inspiration in our app? It's available on both the iOS App Store and Google Play. And for those that prefer to listen to me read articles, you can pop over to Spotify or our website.
Happy Reading!

IndieAuthorMagazin

I0106247

STORYTELLER
OPERATING SYSTEM

NOTION FOR AUTHORS

LEARN:

The PARA Method for Writers
Building Your Story Bible
Setting up Books and Series
Task Management for Writing
Task Management for Editing, ARCs, and Betas
Collaborating in Notion
Incorporating Other Apps into Notion
Automating Workflows
And More!

SIGN UP: INDIEAUTHORTRAINING.COM

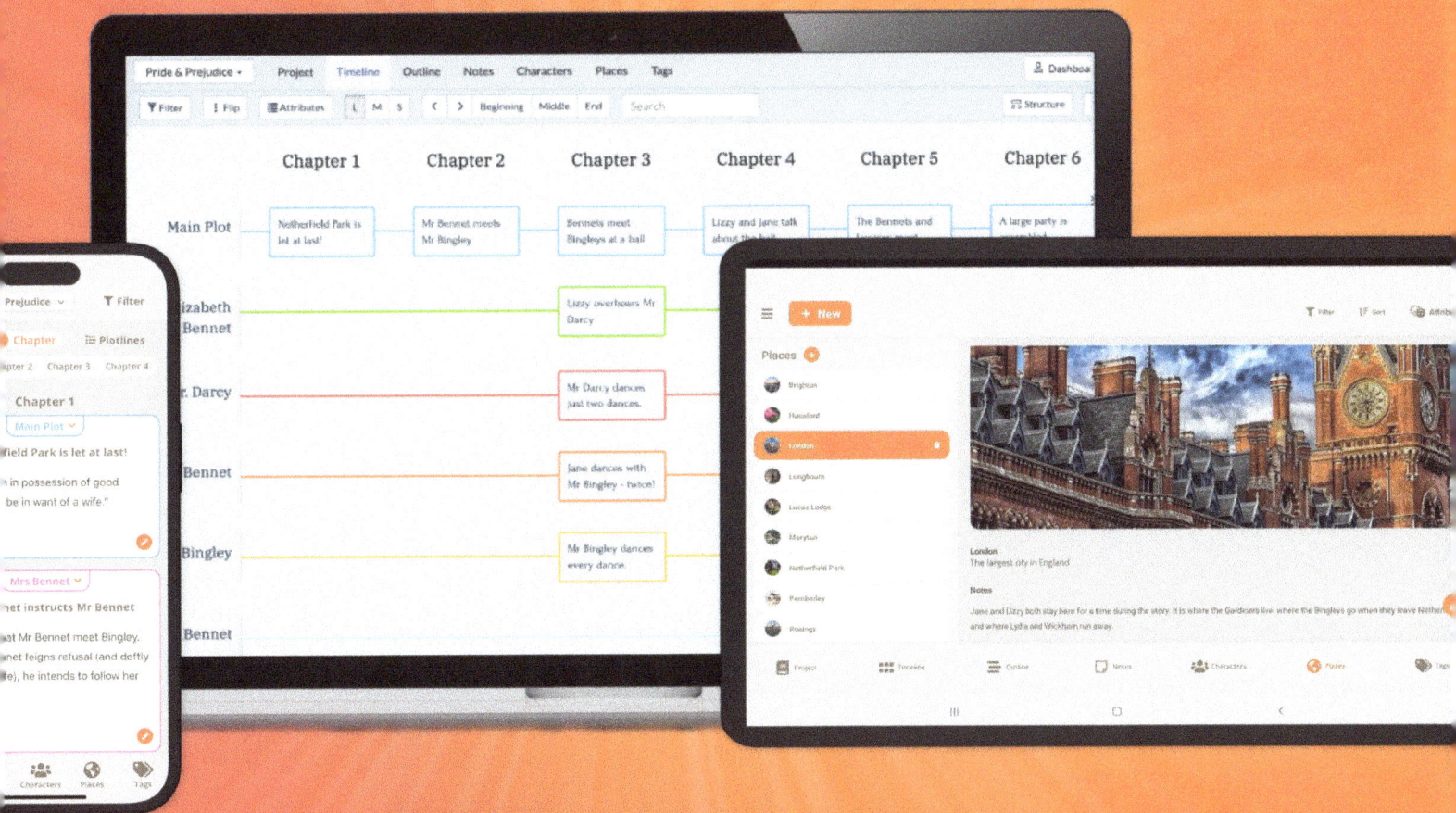

> I joined while having a crisis with Amazon KDP… The Alliance is a beacon of light. I recommend that all indie authors join…
> **Susan Marshall**

> The Alliance is about standing together.
> **Joanna Penn**

> It's the good stuff, all on one place.
> **Richard Wright**

> "ALLi has helped me in myriad ways: discounts on services, vetting providers, charting a course to sales success. But more than anything it's a community of friendly, knowledgeable, helpful people."
> **Beth Duke**

See hundreds more testimonials at:
AllianceIndependentAuthors.org/testimonials

IAM
ORGANIC TRAFFIC

Authorpreneurs in Action

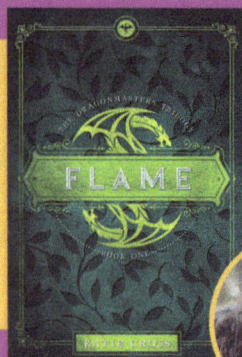

"I love Lulu! They've been a fantastic distributor of my paperbacks and an excellent partner as I dive into direct sales. They integrate so smoothly with my personal Shopify store, and their customer support has been top notch."

Katie Cross, katiecrossbooks.com

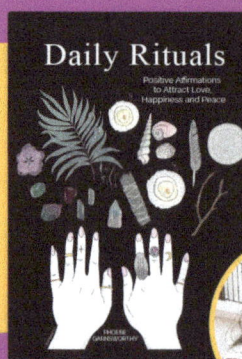

"Having my own store has given me the freedom to look at my creativity as a profitable business and lifelong career."

Phoebe Garnsworthy, phoebegarnsworthy.com

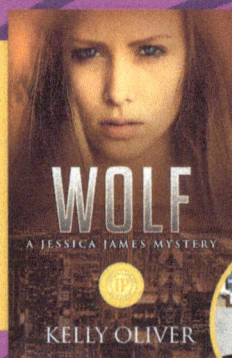

"Lulu has a super handy integration with Shopify. Lulu makes it so easy to sell paperbacks directly to readers."

Kelly Oliver, kellyoliverbooks.com

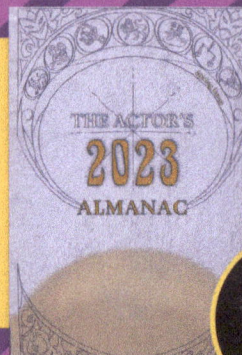

"My experience with Lulu Direct has been more convenient and simple than I anticipated or thought possible. I simply publish, take a step back and allow the well-oiled machine to run itself. Most grateful!"

Molly McGivern, theactorsalmanac.com

INDIE
AUTHOR MAGAZINE

EDITORIAL

Publisher | Chelle Honiker

Editor in Chief | Nicole Schroeder

Creative Director | Alice Briggs

Partner Relationship Manager | Elaine Bateman

ADVERTISING & MARKETING

Inquiries
Ads@AtheniaCreative.com

Information
Partner.IndieAuthorMagazine.com

CONTRIBUTORS

Angela Archer, Elaine Bateman, Bradley Charbonneau, Jackie Dana, Heather Clement Davis, Jamie Davis, Laurel Decher, Gill Fernley, Jen B. Green, Marion Hermannsen, Jenn Lessmann, Megan Linski-Fox, Angie Martin, Merri Maywether, Kevin McLaughlin, Jenn Mitchell, Tanya Nellestein, Susan Odev, Eryka Parker, Tiffany Robinson, Robyn Sarty, Joe Solari, David Viergutz

SUBSCRIPTIONS
https://indieauthormagazine.com/subscribe/

HOW TO READ
https://indieauthormagazine.com/how-to-read/

WHEN WRITING MEANS BUSINESS
IndieAuthorMagazine.com

Athenia Creative | 6820 Apus Dr., Sparks, NV, 89436 USA | 775.298.1925
ISSN 2768-7880 (online)–ISSN 2768-7872 (print)

As much as I'd like to say otherwise, there is no guidebook for being an indie author. I'll admit, it would be a great way to market this magazine. But the same freedom that drove so many to explore our industry means every one of us approaches our business differently than the next. We're authors; we write our own guidebooks.

As we reach the middle of the unofficial author events season, the fact that so many of us forge our own paths makes it easy to see why conferences and workshops are so popular. They're amazing for building community and connecting us with others who speak our language. Where else can you introduce yourself by your genre or outline a short story over dinner? They're also a chance for us to learn about what's been done, what hasn't, what's worked for others, and what mistakes we can avoid repeating. They still allow us to find our own paths, but they give us flashlights to light our way and introduce us to friends who will tell us to keep going when the road ahead is foggy.

Events aren't the only place to find this support, however. Help and friendship are everywhere in our industry, if you know where to look. In this issue, we're introducing you to Indie Author Training (https://indieauthortraining.com), the newest sister site to *Indie Author Magazine* and one such gathering place for authors. As you'll read in the feature by Karen Guyler, Indie Author Training's director of community and content, the platform is a marketplace for courses, product tours, live webinars, or a chance to converse with other authors. "It's a beacon for those navigating the indie publishing landscape," according to the website, no matter what path you've chosen or how long you've been mapping it.

We hope that beacon will shine a light on the right path for your author journey. I, for one, can't wait to see where it leads you.

Nicole Schroeder
Editor in Chief
Indie Author Magazine

Nicole Schroeder is a storyteller at heart. As the editor in chief of Indie Author Magazine, she brings nearly a decade of journalism and editorial experience to the publication, delighting in any opportunity to tell true stories and help others do the same. She holds a bachelor's degree from the Missouri School of Journalism and minors in English and Spanish. Her previous work includes editorial roles at local publications, and she's helped edit and produce numerous fiction and nonfiction books, including a Holocaust survivor's memoir, alongside independent publishers. Her own creative writing has been published in national literary magazines. When she's not at her writing desk, Nicole is usually in the saddle, cuddling her guinea pigs, or spending time with family. She loves any excuse to talk about Marvel movies and considers National Novel Writing Month its own holiday.

School's in Session

A DEEP DIVE INTO IAM'S NEW COMMUNITY-FOCUSED EDUCATION PLATFORM, INDIE AUTHOR TRAINING

The world of indie publishing is an exhilarating adventure, but it can also feel like you're navigating constantly shifting terrain. New tools emerge daily, promising to streamline workflows, boost productivity, and propel your self-publishing journey. But where do you, the busy indie author, find the time and resources to stay informed and equipped? Enter Indie Author Training, the innovative sister site of *Indie Author Magazine* designed to be your one-stop shop for mastering the ever-evolving realm of indie author technology.

The trusted team behind *Indie Author Magazine*, which has remained committed to providing unbiased information and supporting the indie author community since its inaugural issue three years ago, brings its same dedication to Indie Author Training, offering a marketplace of courses, product tours, and live webinars on every aspect of managing a publishing business, plus a range of other features. Here, we'll delve deeper into the platform, exploring how it's empowering authors to learn, connect, and thrive.

WEBINARS: A MULTIFACETED APPROACH TO LEARNING

Indie Author Training's dynamic webinar series caters to the diverse needs of indie authors through a multifaceted approach to learning. Here's what you can expect.

- **Emerging New Tech:** In-depth sessions on new platforms showcase tech tools designed to free you up to focus on the heart of your passion—writing. Learn how these tools can streamline your workflow, from manuscript organization to formatting and distribution. See platforms in action and discover how they can empower you to get back to weaving your magic on the page.

- **In-Depth Analysis with Industry Experts:** The world of indie publishing is constantly bombarded with new information and trends. Indie Author Training cuts through the noise by offering insightful webinars-

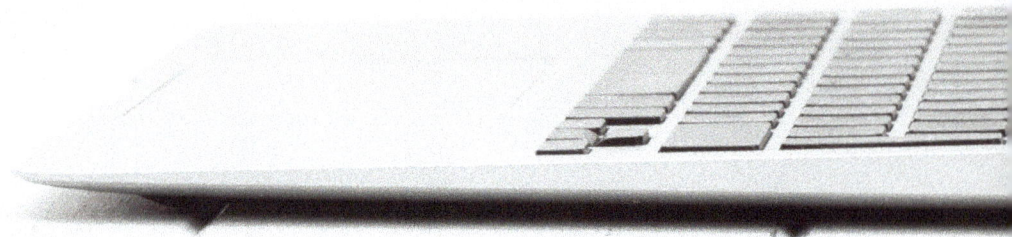

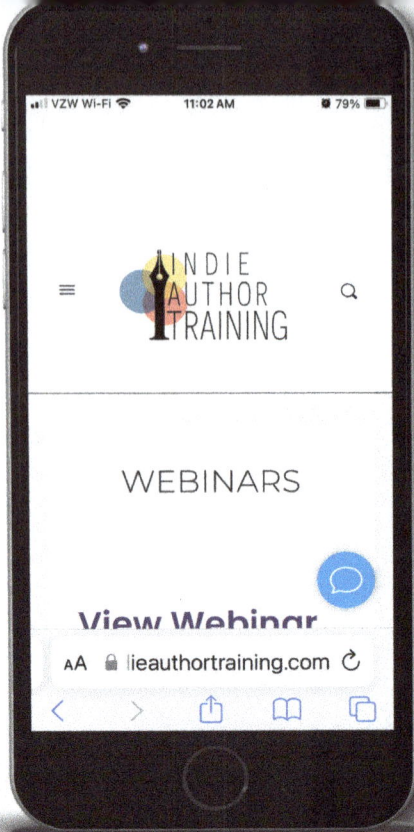

featuring established industry figures. These experts provide well-researched and balanced perspectives on crucial aspects of self-publishing, from the evolving landscape of marketing strategies to the nuanced functionalities of specific publishing platforms. Gain a comprehensive understanding from trusted voices to guide your decision-making and refine your self-publishing approach.

- **Build a Sustainable Indie Author Career:** Feeling overwhelmed by the constant pressure to optimize your workflow? The "Sustainable Career Tips" series explores innovative and research-backed strategies for building a long-lasting and fulfilling indie author career. These sessions delve into topics like work-life balance, incorporating healthy habits into your routine, and fostering a creative mindset for long-term success. Learn unconventional approaches that can help you unlock your full potential while prioritizing your well-being along your author journey.

PRODUCT TOURS: DEMYSTIFYING YOUR TECH TOOLBOX

The sheer volume of tech tools available for indie authors can be overwhelming. Indie Author Training simplifies the process with product tours tailored to address specific needs in your creative journey. These comprehensive sessions showcase various tools in action, giving you a clear picture of their functionalities and how they can integrate seamlessly into your existing workflow. Here are some examples you might encounter.

- **Writing Powerhouses:** Delve into the functionalities of writing software like Scrivener and Atticus. Learn how these tools can streamline your outlining, manuscript organization, and editing processes, empowering you to craft compelling narratives with greater efficiency.
- **Grammar Guardians:** Unsure about comma placement or struggling with phrasing? Indie Author Training explores how grammar checkers like ProWritingAid can help you refine your prose and ensure your manuscript shines.
- **Design Decoded:** With the magic of design tools like Canva, you can discover how to create stunning visuals for your book covers, social media posts, and marketing materials. These tools can elevate your brand identity and attract your target audience.

- **Content Creation Companions:** Feeling stuck on that next blog post or social media caption? Explore how AI-powered writing assistants like ChatGPT, Claude, or Sudowrite can spark inspiration and help you overcome writer's block. These innovative tools can help you generate fresh ideas and refine your process for content creation.
- **Email Marketing Essentials:** Building a loyal reader base is crucial for indie author success. Whether you prefer Mailchimp, MailerLite, ConvertKit, or another email service provider, Indie Author Training will guide you through the features. Learn how to connect with your readers, craft engaging newsletters, and build a thriving online community.

This is not an exhaustive list. Indie Author Training is constantly exploring and introducing you to a vast array of tools to propel your indie author success, and more product tours are added to the site regularly as free and paid content.

Digital Fore Edge Design
for Print on Demand

Scan to learn
more now

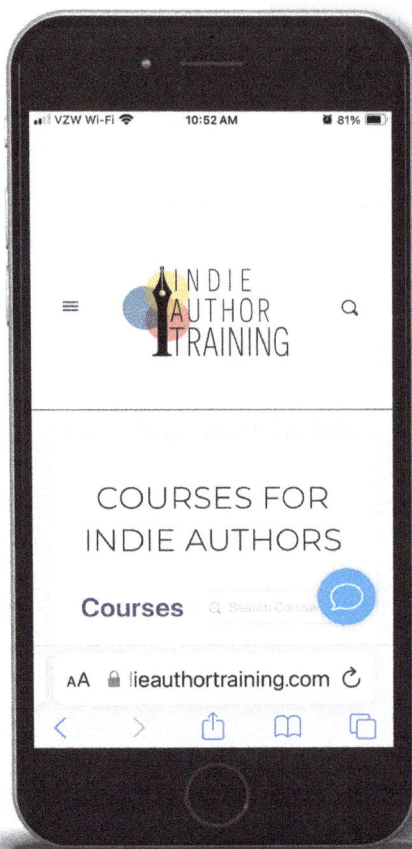

COURSE LIBRARY: A MARKETPLACE OF EXPERTISE

Forget the days of limited learning options. Indie Author Training's course library is a dynamic marketplace for knowledge, meticulously curated to empower your indie author journey. Here's how this innovative platform elevates your learning experience.

• **Learn from the Best:** Step beyond the confines of a single instructor. Indie Author Training functions as a marketplace, connecting you with a diverse range of industry leaders. Instructors set their own pricing, structure, and schedule, allowing them to tailor their courses to offer in-depth, practical guidance. Acclaimed authors, editors, marketing specialists, and publishing professionals bring their unique perspectives and proven strategies to the table. Whether you crave insights on crafting captivating narratives or mastering the intricacies of self-publishing platforms, you'll find a course led by a recognized expert who aligns with your specific needs.

• **Masterful Delivery, Lasting Impact:** Exceptional instruction goes beyond just content. Indie Author Training understands this and uses a state-of-the-art learning management system (LMS) equipped with a robust suite of tools designed to enhance your learning. Interactive modules, engaging quizzes, downloadable resources, and collaborative forums are all crafted by instructional design professionals.

• **Structured Learning beyond Lectures:** Indie Author Training's courses aren't just passive lectures. Instructors have designed clear learning paths and a structured environment, allowing you to progress at your own pace and ensuring you have space to develop a deeper understanding of the material before moving on to new concepts. Instructors may also offer templates, checklists, or software tutorials to enhance your learning experience and equip you with the resources to implement your newfound knowledge.

• **Dive Deep into Specific Skills:** Whether you're looking to craft captivating email newsletters that build a loyal reader base or leverage the power of platforms like Amazon ads and Facebook Ads to reach a wider audience, Indie Author Training has a course tailored to your needs. Expand your marketing expertise with courses like "Google Rich Results and Ads," or delve into the world of AI writing assistants with "ChatGPT Basics." Sharpen your storytelling skills by exploring the nuances of tropes, or learn the basics of editing. New courses are added every week, and anyone can make suggestions for new instructors or course topics.

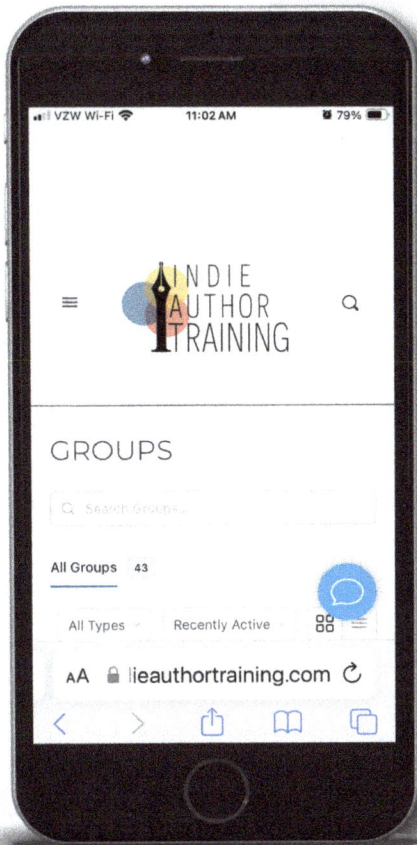

DISCUSSION GROUPS: FOSTERING A SUPPORTIVE COMMUNITY

The journey of an indie author can be isolating. Indie Author Training fosters a vibrant community through its discussion groups. These safe spaces provide a platform for you to connect with fellow authors, ask questions, and share experiences, and they offer other key benefits as well.

• **Unwavering Support:** Discussion groups offer a supportive environment free from the whims of ever-changing social media algorithms. Here, you can voice your concerns, seek guidance, and connect directly with authors who understand the unique challenges and triumphs of the self-publishing journey. Gain encouragement, share your experiences, and learn from the successes and struggles of others in the indie author community.

• **In-Depth Discussions:** Groups on Indie Author Training allow you to delve deeper into specific topics and tech tools without searching. Whether you're stuck on a specific aspect of marketing or seeking inspiration for your next project, forums provide a breeding ground for collaboration and shared knowledge. Learn from the collective wisdom of the community, troubleshoot challenges, and discover innovative approaches to navigate your self-publishing journey.

• **Direct Access to Experts:** For courses offered through Indie Author Training, dedicated discussion groups provide a platform to interact directly with the course instructors. This personalized access allows you to gain further insights and clarify any lingering doubts. Ask questions, receive feedback on your work, and benefit from the expertise of the instructors in a focused environment.

By combining informative webinars, insightful product tours, comprehensive courses, and a thriving discussion forum, Indie Author Training empowers indie authors to navigate the ever-evolving landscape of self-publishing. Indie Author Training is always open to suggestions for new topics and tools to cover. Head over to https://indieauthortraining. com, create your free account, and embark on a successful journey as an indie author. ■

Karen Guyler

Karen Guyler

Always being the new girl at nine schools on two continents was no fun at all so books became the only constant in Karen Guyler's life, even if they didn't help her get out of sports days. Now settled in Milton Keynes, England, Britain's best kept secret, she juggles reading with writing twisty thrilling stories, her children, husband and two grand-puppies – a much nicer mix!
She also teaches Creative Writing for Adult Education with lots of laughter in amongst the word wrangling and discovery.

Indie Author Training Roundup

If there's one thing we can be certain of in our indie author careers, it's that things change constantly, and trying to keep up can be a real time sink. But how can you progress, streamline, and enhance your career when you don't know what you don't know? That's where our sister site, Indie Author Training, comes in, a one-stop place that offers education, community, and tools for storytellers.

Our kick-off series of webinars in April, hosted by *IAM*'s publisher, Chelle Honiker, covered topics such as AI use cases, direct sales for indie authors, and an introduction to Zapier and its potential to revolutionize your marketing strategies.

In our webinar on time management, Honiker talked about using ultradian rhythms when batching and time blocking and gave examples of apps and software that can help streamline your writing time. In our outside-the-box thinking webinar, Indie Author Training's Karen Guyler presented ideas for incorporating health and wellness in your writing regime, from the 20-20-20 rule to exercise snacking to stimulate your thought processes. You can check out the replays at https://indieauthortraining.com/webinars/time-management-for-indie-authors and https://indieauthortraining.com/webinars/outside-the-box-thinking-for-indie-authors.

In May we welcomed Romance author Ines Johnson's first Trope of the Month webinar on hidden identity. Learn all about this narrative goldmine that combines mystery and suspense, as well as the universal quest for true love and self-discovery, at the replay here: https://indieauthortraining.com/webinars/hidden-identity-trope-with-ines-johnson. Johnson will be back with another trope soon.

We're finalizing the webinars for this coming month, so rush over to https://indieauthortraining.com/webinars to see what will help you in your career.

In our discussion groups, the author accountability discussion on the productivity thread has been especially popular. This is a low-input, quasi-anonymous way to help you be accountable to yourself with the added bonus of cheerleading, if that motivates you. Check it out at https://indieauthortraining.com/groups/productivity/forum/topic/author-accountability.

New webinars, courses, and product tours are coming online every week, and our discussion groups are always open for members to chat with one another, ask questions of thought leaders in the industry, and share tips without being subject to the whims of an algorithm. You can create an account for free at https://indieauthortraining.com/register. ■

Karen Guyler

From the Stacks

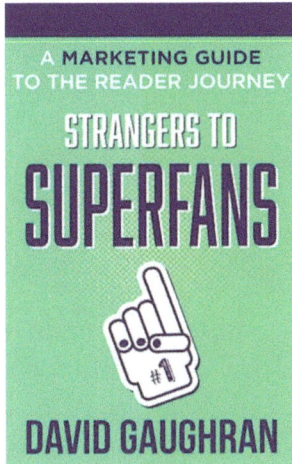

Strangers to Superfans: A Marketing Guide to The Reader Journey
https://books2read.com/Superfans

David Gaughran is a seasoned self-published author who has used his expertise to coach countless indies to success through his workshops, blog, and Let's Get Publishing series. His marketing guide *Strangers to Superfans* is no exception, illuminating the five stages of "the reader journey" and sharing how to optimize each one to boost sales and build fans for life. Beyond simply sharing best practices, Gaughran also highlights potential pitfalls in the process and how you can get out of them, making it useful for authors at any point in their marketing journey.

Google Trends
https://trends.google.com/trends

Whether you're looking to refresh your metadata or trying to pick keywords for social media posts, it's helpful to know what people are searching and which terms are most likely to drive traffic where you want it to go. Google Trends offers a real-time look at what people are looking for online, as well as historical data on where and when searches for a particular word or phrase peaked—plus, it's just fun to explore. You can also sign up to receive a daily newsletter of trending topics delivered to your inbox.

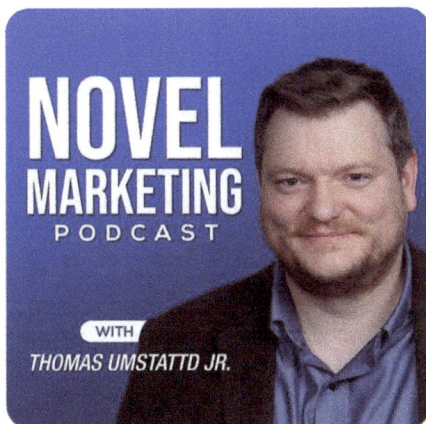

Novel Marketing Podcast
https://www.authormedia.com/novel-marketing

Novel Marketing is the longest-running author marketing podcast in the world, featuring advice for both self-published and traditionally published authors on growing their platform, increasing sales, and finding new superfans among their readers. Host and Author Media CEO Thomas Umstattd Jr. interviews a range of authors and publishing industry experts, sharing proven tips and strategies to growing your book business in a new episode each week.

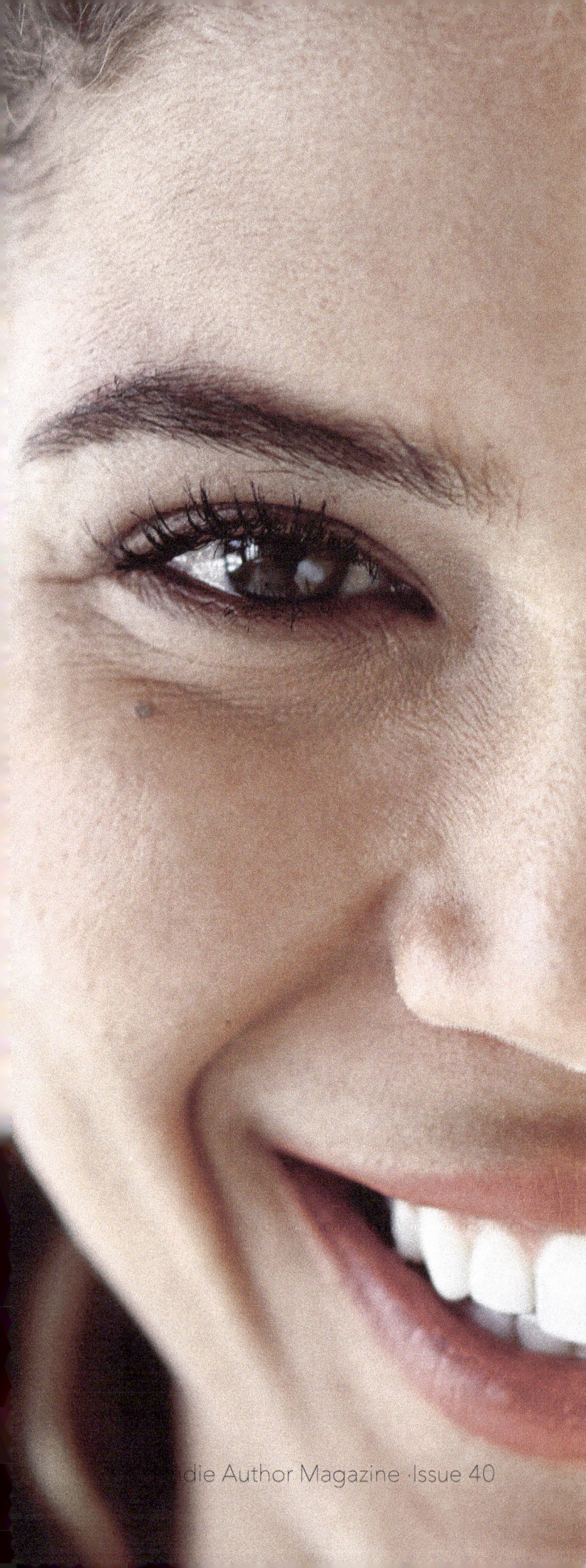

ALLI EXCLUSIVE

All Eyes on Your Author Business

We're probably all familiar with paid advertising meant to drive readers to a website or other platforms, called "traffic." But before investing in ads, authors should optimize for unpaid, organic traffic.

For most authors, organic traffic is generated in three ways:

- **organic search:** Visits coming through search engines, such as readers searching for your author name or book title;
- **organic social:** Traffic coming from unadvertised posts on social media platforms like Facebook, Instagram, X, TikTok, YouTube, or Goodreads; and
- **events:** Traffic coming from your author or book events, online and off.

These depend on effective search engine optimization (SEO). When optimized, each can be a powerful way of building your following, reaching new readers, and staying connected with your current fans.

To capitalize on the benefits organic traffic can bring, you need to be willing to invest not dollars but time to understand the SEO landscape, optimize your platforms, and continue to refine your metadata over time.

So how do you encourage those visitors to come to your site?

Whatever stage you're at as a self-publishing author, the Alliance of Independent Authors (ALLi) can help you ensure you're signposting visitor pathways to your online presences correctly and clearly.

BEGINNER AUTHORS: OPTIMIZE YOUR ONLINE HOME BASE

Optimizing your website for organic search is very similar to optimizing your metadata on retail platforms. Those platforms' algorithms rely on your book title, author name, genres and subgenres, keywords, and categories to point the right readers to your books.

In the same way indie authors can tweak their books' metadata to optimize clicks, reads, and sales, you can tweak your website's metadata to optimize its effectiveness. Include terms in your website that will lead the right people to it. Writing Suspense? Be sure the word "suspense" and other related terms are included on your site. Targeting recent retirees? Include that explicitly on your site.

Revise and refresh your data so that the site doesn't appear "stale" to search engines. A regular blog post or podcast page is a great way to do this. If you don't blog or podcast, add new pages and change things up regularly.

If you're building your website yourself—perhaps via an easy-to-use website builder—this will be easy to do. If you have someone build your site for you, make sure they have the expertise needed to implement SEO and that they are familiar enough with the author business that they will be able to do this effectively.

Even if someone else builds your website, you should be able to modify it for SEO since you don't want to have to go back to the developer every time you want to tweak your data.

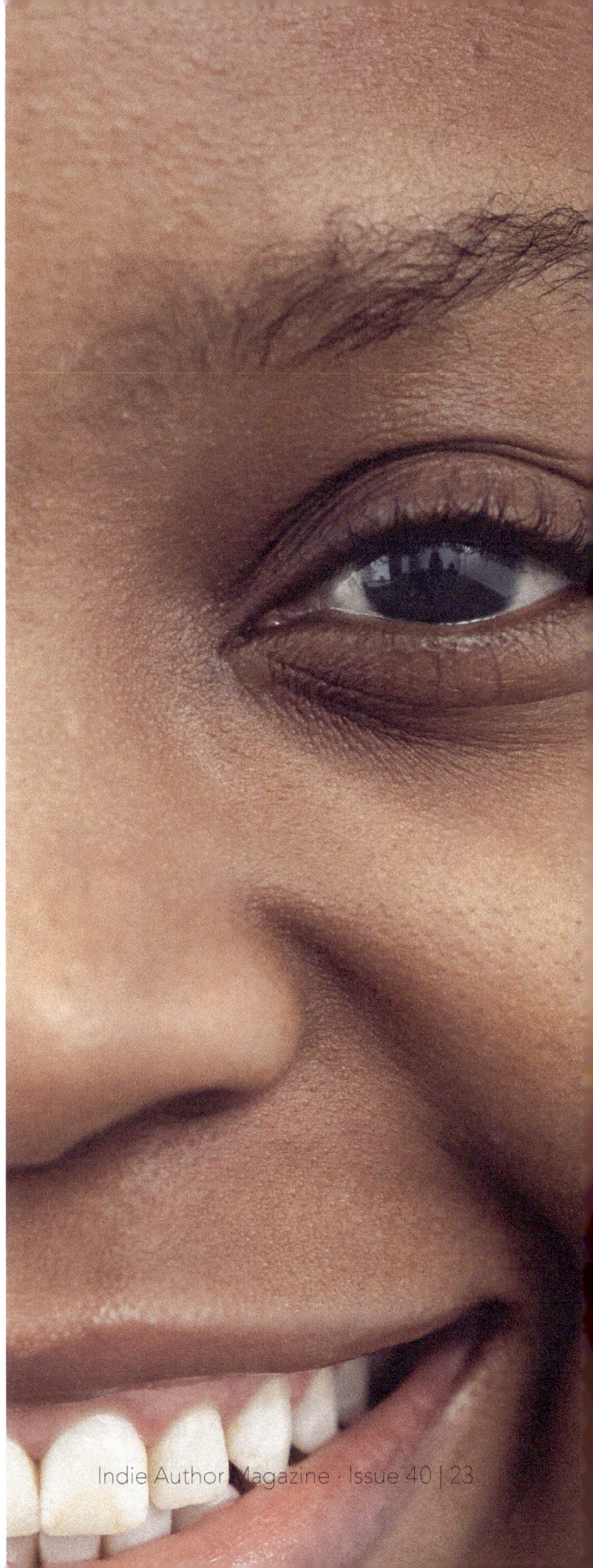

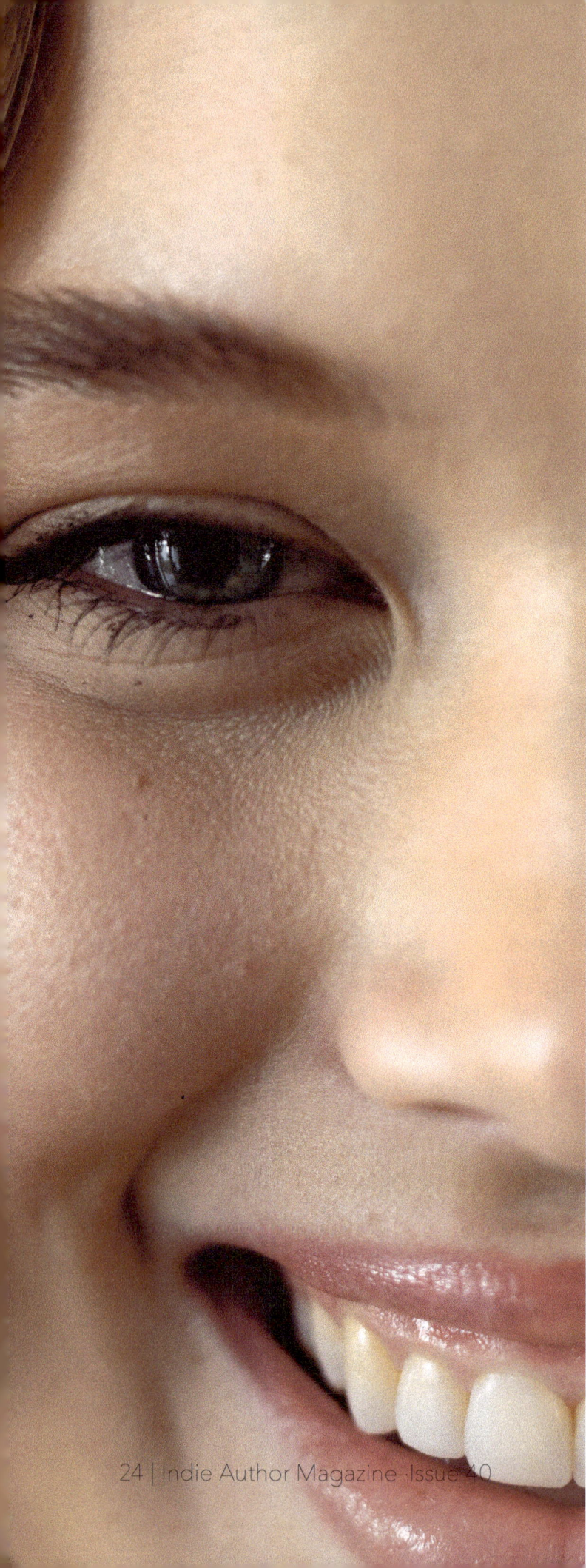

As with book metadata, results won't be immediate; it takes some time for search engines to find and reflect new data.

You'll find lots of information about how to implement SEO in these easy-to-follow ALLi guides:

- https://selfpublishingadvice.org/seo-for-indie-authors
- https://selfpublishingadvice.org/improve-author-website-seo-tips
- https://selfpublishingadvice.org/seo-for-authors
- https://selfpublishingadvice.org/book-meta-data-keywords-and-amazon-category-changes

EMERGING AUTHORS: LEAVE NO READER UNLINKED

If you've taken the steps needed to implement SEO effectively on your website, as described above, consider other platforms you can optimize, such as social media.

Do all your social media posts include hashtags, alt text for images, and a link back to your chosen destination? Even email offers an opportunity for organic traffic; do you have an email signature that includes a clickable link to your website and your primary social media platforms?

Make it as easy as possible for anyone to find you and your work online. Leave no reader unlinked!

Calls-to-action (CTAs) are often an important part of social optimization. Use ALLi's guide to ensure you're including the right calls to action on your website and social: https://selfpublishingadvice.org/calls-to-action.

EXPERIENCED AUTHORS: RETRACE YOUR STEPS AND BRING IN THE EXPERTS

Optimizing for organic traffic is not a once-and-done activity, so even experienced authors need to revisit their SEO data and practices periodically. Take some time to retrace your steps regularly and check that your SEO is in good shape.

As your sales grow, seek opportunities for relevant and trustworthy sites to link back to you, thus raising your search engine status. High authority sites like TV and radio channels, mainstream media, and popular blogs and podcasts have the most weight.

If you have some budget and feel your SEO game needs sharpening, consider bringing in an SEO expert to update your core site and teach you a few key skills to further lift your visibility. Ensure anyone you work with has experience with books and authors, so they can focus their attentions on the right audience.

Building organic traffic requires time and ongoing commitment, but it offers a good return on your time investment by helping readers more easily find you and your books. ■

Matty Dalrymple, ALLi Campaigns Manager

Matty Dalrymple, ALLi Campaigns Manager

The Alliance of Independent Authors (ALLi) is a global membership association for self-publishing authors. A non-profit, our mission is ethics and excellence in self-publishing. Everyone on our team is a working indie author and we offer advice and advocacy for self-publishing authors within the literary, publishing and creative industries around the world. www.allianceindependentauthors.org

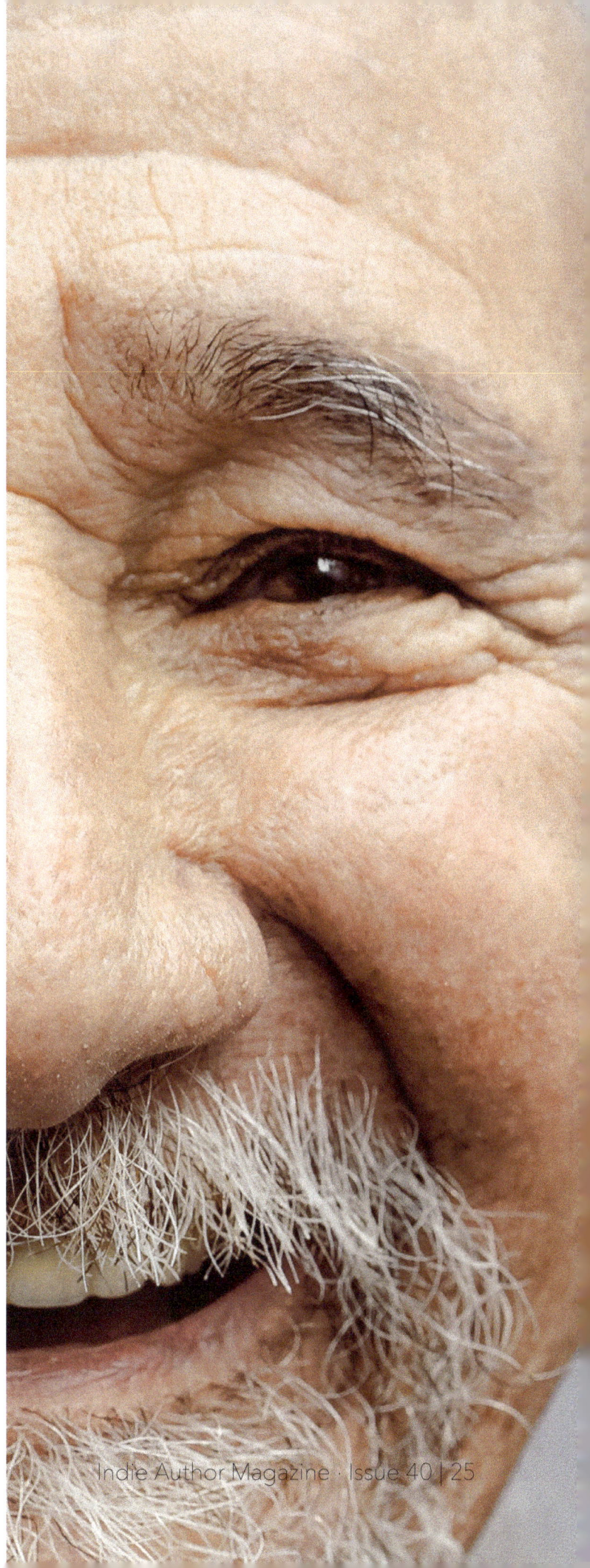

Dear Indie Annie,

I like to think I've conquered impostor syndrome, but any time I give interviews, reach out to someone with a research question, or try to set up local author events, I feel awkward and out of place. How do I confidently approach professionals outside the author community?

Out of My Element

Dear Out of My Element,

My dear elemental friend, reaching beyond our cozy author circles can indeed feel as precarious as a hobbit venturing into the wilds without Gandalf. All those big co-marketing events, media interviews, and research convos can feel like you're stumbling ill prepared into an orc den. How's a gentle book nerd to navigate?

Just like Frodo and friends, you simply must muster bravery and plunge into those unknown territories. After all, what's an epic adventure without testing your courage or trusting in the offered help of a friendly elf?

I have been around this author block a few times, and the one constant complaint I hear in the snug tea rooms and neon-lit bars fellow authors inhabit is that every one of us battles impostor syndrome—even those seemingly confident six- and seven-figure authors whose beautiful, smiling faces grace the cover of this illustrious tome.

We all inevitably face the same questions and doubts. Will the next book fail? Will my fans accept my new direction? Has Amazon confused my royalties with someone else's? And no one enjoys public speaking! I defy anyone to tell me differently. The most seasoned professional entertainers talk of feeling butterflies in their stomachs before every show.

Therein, my dear, lies the point. You feel nauseated and unsteady because you care. You are cautious because you are a good person and do not wish to offend. You are a writer because you are sensitive and passionate, and these traits, though excellent assets in any character, make you a prime candidate for nerves and insecurities.

So how do you manage it? First, prepare yourself like the fellowship readying for departure from Rivendell. Study up on who you'll be

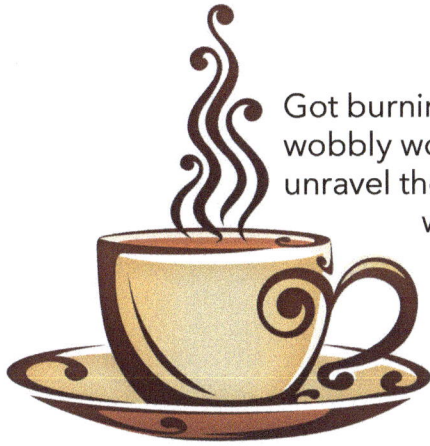

Got burning questions about the wibbly-wobbly world of indie authoring? Eager to unravel the mysteries of publishing, writing woes, or anything in between? Give your quizzical quills a whirl and shoot your musings over to indieannie@indieauthormagazine.com. Your inky quandaries are my cup of tea!

encountering and their ways. Are they Hollywood hotshots or university intellectuals? If you're giving an interview, brush up on proper etiquette and likely interests, so you can engage confidently. If you're signing up for an event, research themes, topics, and what makes that event unique in the marketplace. Ask yourself how you will add value to those attending.

Next, assemble your own trusty company of allies. Consult wise mentors—other authors, perhaps—who have trod similar paths before. What counsel do they offer? Recruit encouraging friends and critique partners as hype hobbits believing in your quest.

Then channel your inner Samwise Gamgee, ever loyal despite trembling in Mordor's shadow. Stay focused on your worthy mission: growing your platform and fanbase by connecting with new audiences. Fake that confidence until it becomes unshakable. We all feel the fear, but as American psychologist and author Susan Jeffers suggests, the secret is to do it anyway.

Frodo had Sam. Who is your biggest cheerleader? Consider what they would say to you whenever you doubt yourself. Nod sagely at their advice and pick up that phone, hit "Send" on that email, or put your best foot forward on that stage. They believe you can do it, and so should you.

And should nerves still jangle, remember even protagonists stumble! The great Luke Skywalker withered under Sith browbeating. Buffy wilted against the toughest Big Bads. Pivotal failures shape the heroes we adore—and those we craft.

So brace yourself, my hobbit friend! While these battles may loom dauntingly, the boons awaiting those who persevere turn them into shire mountains worth scaling. Trust your courage, and commence your calling!

Over Hiccup Hill and Underhill,
Happy writing,
Indie Annie
X

10 TIPS FOR
LANDING LOCAL MEDIA APPEARANCES

In today's interconnected world, authors have many opportunities to promote their reading and autograph events. Leveraging local radio, event listings, newspapers, and social media can enhance your visibility and attract a larger audience. By utilizing these media outlets, authors can transform their in-person events into anticipated gatherings, ensuring their stories reach a broader, more engaged audience.

Media outlets don't have to be big for their stories to have an impact on your event's success. Come explore ten tips for how authors can harness the power of media to support and elevate their reading events.

1 ATTRACT ATTENTION WITH PRESS RELEASES

Writing and sending press releases can generate coverage in newspapers, online publications, and broadcast media. A well-crafted press release can catch the attention of journalists looking for local interest stories and provide you with free publicity for the event. Keep your release short and to the point, including any necessary information and a hook that explains why your event is worth covering. Have one main URL for people to follow, and include contact information in case a journalist has follow-up questions. Make sure you include a graphic for your event with the release.

Pro Tip: You can write releases for free, but if you have a small budget, choose a budget-friendly paid option to get a more targeted service for your event. Here are a few options to explore.

24-7 Press Release
https://24-7pressrelease.com
With plans starting at $29, authors use this service to announce their books at launch. It could also announce your reading events.

PR.com
https://pr.com
Plans start at $60. Authors and event coordinators use this service to promote their events.

PRfree
https://prfree.org
Plans start for free or at a low cost. This service is more limited in scope than the paid PR companies, but it is budget friendly for authors with little PR capital.

PR Log
https://prlog.org
This company is well known and offers free press releases. You can upgrade and pay for more targeted services.

2 OPEN YOUR GLOSSY PAGES

Appearing in local lifestyle or cultural magazines can help authors reach a niche audience. If you write memoirs, seek family journals. For nonfiction, find magazines that cover your topic of interest. If you write fiction, discover magazines that include author interviews or book reviews along with their stories. You may find an opportunity there if you are a good match for the magazine's typical subject matter. Ask whether you can collaborate with the magazine to write a piece about your book's theme or participate in an interview, providing details about your upcoming readings.

3 BE FOUND IN THE LIBRARY

Partnering with local libraries for book readings and discussions can draw in a crowd. Libraries often promote events through their newsletters, social media, and community boards, providing additional promotional support. To book your event, approach the head librarian and pitch your event idea. If the library has a conference room or other open location, it could be a great place to hold a reading. Often, your local library will host book fairs or other literary events as well, or it will sponsor online events. These can be great ways to draw a larger crowd of new readers and a valuable resource when searching for a location to host your author event.

Pro Tip: While libraries will do a small amount of marketing for your event, be sure you're promoting it in your own channels as well. If you are given a time slot for your event or join one of their book festivals, promote it as you would for any other location.

4 DELIVER YOUR NEWS BY EMAIL

Consider segmenting your email list and creating a separate list of readers close to your area so you can send additional emails to your local fans without posting to your entire list. This can be profitable as you develop in-person events at bookstores, libraries, and other reading venues.

As you host events in your local area, be sure to designate these in-person signups as local. Mention your events in your regular newsletter and email blasts, as well as to this list, to encourage people to attend. Plan to announce well before the event, with an additional quick reminder just before it takes place. Offering an incentive, such as a free chapbook, a special sticker, or a flier, can also entice your readers. These attendees will be your most dedicated readers and potentially the most excited about the chance to meet you at your in-person event.

5 JOIN THE ULTIMATE BLOG JOURNEY

Collaborating with local bloggers to write guest posts or give interviews can create buzz around a new book release or author event, attracting a wider audience within your community. Plan to schedule appearances on a blog tour well before your book launch. Have the bulk of your appearances drop around the time of your launch, but scatter more in the next few months to follow as well. Many times, you will find calls from bloggers looking for authors to feature on their sites. Other times, you can find services who will set up a tour for you. When you set up your blog tour, if you also have in-person events scheduled, you can ask each blogger on the tour to include it at the bottom of their review or interview. Many times, they will accommodate you.

6 FIND LOCAL EVENTS AT YOUR FINGERTIPS

Submitting event details to local event apps can reach tech-savvy community members. These apps often allow users to search for events by date and type, making it easier for people to discover your reading without it getting buried by other community events. Be certain to list your event in as many apps as you can to get the word out. They are often free to use and will be targeted to those in your community who are already looking for a fun activity. Many community directors, museums, and libraries also have event pages where you can connect with your local community and get the word out about your event.

Pro Tip: In addition to searching community websites for places to submit your own events, here are a few event listing services to consider:

Eventbrite
https://eventbrite.com
Eventbrite is an event ticketing service that includes a discovery calendar. You can set up an event for free for up to twenty-five tickets. If you want to promote to a larger group, the pay scale starts at $9 per one hundred tickets, with prices increasing in increments of $10 for larger events.

Meetup
https://meetup.com
As a free member of Meetup, you can find venues to host book events or start a single group of your own for free. If you find Meetup works for you, the standard subscription and pro plan offer additional features, including the ability to create more groups or set event fees or membership dues.

Facebook Events
https://facebook.com/events
Placing your event on Facebook is free and will tap into the people in your own network, as well as those in your local community. When planning your own author event, consider filling out an event form with your personal account so your friends and family will see the event on their feed as well.

---

7 ENGAGE LOCAL INFLUENCERS

Partnering with local influencers or social media personalities can amplify an author's event promotion and marketing for a new release. These movers and shakers are part of every community. Find ones that are keyed into the area where you wish to hold your event and partner with them.

A simple way to locate them is to use Google. Type in "[city name] + influencers" and a list of people will appear. Similar to group promotions and newsletter swaps in the author world, an influencer hosting you on their TikTok or Instagram may be a boost to their reach while also helping you set the stage for your author event. Have a pitch ready, and message influencers as you learn of them.

---

8 TUNE INTO PODCASTS

Many communities have local or niche podcasts, and listeners often appreciate the in-depth discussions that podcasts allow, which can translate into a more engaged audience at live events. Calls for podcasts appear all the time in Facebook Groups, on X, on Bluesky, on Mastodon, or on other social media platforms. Create an elevator pitch about what benefits you would bring as a podcast guest and author. Take some time to research local podcasts and scroll through recent posts to find interview opportunities. When you spot a likely match, direct-message an inquiry to the producer.

Another way to find interviews is to sign up for a podcast matching service. The service works similarly to a dating service, pairing podcasters with potential guests and vice versa. These services usually have a free option for you to try out the program and see if it is worthwhile. Find a list of services to explore in "Unlocking the Power of Podcast Appearances for Authors" in *IAM*'s March 2024 issue.

9 AIR YOUR STORY ON COMMUNITY TV

Many communities have public access TV channels that welcome local content. Authors can create short segments about their books and events to be aired on these channels, reaching viewers who prefer local programming.

To become a public access producer and gain access to the channel's time, you will need to register as a local resident and attend a production class. This certifies you on their equipment and gives you the basic skills you need to produce programming. You will then be encouraged to create thirty-minute to sixty-minute programs to air on the channel.

Many times, a public access producer is already producing a book show. They are easier to access than a public television station since they are members of your community; consider reaching out to see if they'd be willing to feature you and your work on their program.

---

10 TALK WITH LOCAL RADIO SHOWS

Public radio often hosts programming on books, poetry, and other cultural topics. Create an elevator pitch about why you should be considered for an interview on these local programs. Prepare engaging stories about yourself as a writer and about the inspiration behind your book.

Pro Tip: Use Google to set up notices for local radio and television stations, as producers will occasionally post calls for appearances. The radio show's website and social media page may also have information on how to apply to be on the show. Sometimes it is helpful to have an agent with connections to secure interviews or book spots in programming, though this may be an investment for newer authors. ■

Wendy Van Camp

Wendy Van Camp

Wendy Van Camp is the Poet Laureate for the City of Anaheim, California. Her work is influenced by cutting edge technology, astronomy, and daydreams. A graduate of the Ad Astra Speculative Fiction Workshop, Wendy is a nominated finalist for the Elgin Award, for the Pushcart Prize, and for a Dwarf Stars Award. Her poems, stories, and articles have appeared in: "Starlight Scifaiku Review", "The Junction", "Quantum Visions", and other literary journals. She is the poet and illustrator of "The Planets: a scifaiku poetry collection" and editor of the annual anthology "Eccentric Orbits: An Anthology of Science Fiction Poetry". Find her at https://wendyvancamp.com

Can I Tell You a Story?

NATALIA HERNANDEZ FOLLOWED THE ORAL TRADITIONS OF HER ANCESTORS INTO A SUCCESSFUL AUTHOR CAREER

Bestselling Fantasy author Natalia Hernandez writes magical Latin American-inspired novels for both YA and adult audiences. But until recently, if you wanted to hear her stories, you had to follow her on TikTok. As a third-culture kid—her mother is Peruvian, and her father is Cuban—she grew up all over the world, so it makes sense that her first audience was worldwide too.

After waking up from a strange dream about prophetic flowers in December 2020, Natalia posted a video about it online, never expecting that her followers would make it go viral. "I made a silly little TikTok skit about it, thinking people would find it funny how wild my dreams are," she says. But her followers were hooked. They started asking what happened next, so she posted skits that expanded the story, dressing up in costumes to differentiate the characters she played. Commenters immediately asked if this story was going to be a book, but she didn't take them seriously until some of them started saying they would write it themselves. She couldn't let that happen.

"Absolutely not. That's my dream, my story," she says. "I think part of it might have been just a little bit of fear and a little bit of spite." It was the final push she needed to move from storytelling on social media to novel writing. She released *The Name-Bearer,* book 1 in her debut series, The Flowers of Prophecy, in 2022.

PUTTING IT DOWN ON PAPER

Natalia grew up hearing Peruvian folklore passed down by her mother from their Incan ancestors. The mythology her mother wove into bedtime stories evolved from a long oral tradition, and in some senses, Natalia has carried that tradition through several "creative-adjacent" career paths, including working as a makeup artist for film and television and at a successful job in product marketing with a skincare company. Although she'd written some unpublished short stories, poetry, and novellas growing up, she never considered writing a full novel. In fact, often when she had a story idea, "instead of sitting down to write it, I would just tell it out loud to someone," she says.

When she decided to write the novel her TikTok followers asked for, she incorporated some of the mythology from her mother's stories. "I did do a lot of research, and I came up with various different versions of typical mythology that I heard. Eventually I had to decide that whatever I was taught was just as valid as whatever someone else was taught across the country. This is my story, and I'm going to be okay with telling it the way my mother told me," she says. Although the novel takes place in a fantasy kingdom, her followers have found its Latin roots relatable and responded enthusiastically to her representation of often marginalized cultures.

Natalia wrote much of her first novel, *The Name-Bearer*, in Guatemala, where she'd lived as a child. Staying with friends, she was energized by the culture and scenery around her. "Waking up and looking out the window and seeing a volcano every morning—you can't help but be inspired by something like that," she says.

As Natalia got further into the book, she continued to post about the story on TikTok, but "the moment that I took it seriously was the day that I stopped posting the skits. I thought, 'Wow, I have enough of a story that it is going to be a novel. I need to not tell everyone the ending,'" she says. Her previous experience in marketing told her to hold back story details from then on, but she needed to continue to nurture the following who'd asked for the story in the first place. So instead of acting out scenes, she began sharing her experiences with writing and her plans to publish. She told followers she expected it to be a trilogy. She has since surprised herself to discover that it will be four books instead of three.

Initially, she considered traditional, small press, and independent publishing equally. She wrote around fifty query letters, receiving feedback "that there was promise, but there was too much Spanish." Other publishers told her she "could have a Latin story or a queer story, but both was too much."

She disagreed.

Knowing that she already had readers interested in her book, and wanting to take strategic advantage of that following, Natalia chose to publish independently. "It was not a deliberate decision, but one of the best things, I think, that could have happened," she says. "I don't think that I would have the cover that I have if I hadn't decided to go independent. I don't think people would be writing me and saying, 'I loved the mentions of the food in the book,' or 'I love that you switched from English to Spanish,' or 'My inner child is healed by reading a Latin Fantasy story.' I think that a lot might have been lost if I had gone any other direction. So I'm really glad that it went the way that it did."

ON CULTURAL REPRESENTATION

Natalia had always been a fan of Fantasy, for many years not even realizing how Eurocentric the genre tends to be. "I think it's one of those things that you don't realize how much it matters until you actually do see yourself represented," she says. She became so accustomed to Fantasy stories taking place with primarily white characters in vaguely medieval settings that early drafts of her own book also followed that pattern. "I didn't even realize that I could write it through my own lens," she says. It wasn't until Natalia read Aiden Thomas's *Cemetery Boys* that she "saw Latin American culture represented in a Fantasy novel. It just opened up my eyes to what the literary world could look like," she says. Once she stopped trying to make her story fit into a Eurocentric framework, the story of The Flowers of Prophecy took on a life of its own.

Natalia extended the Latin American influences from the story to the cover, insisting on an indigenous woman in the design. Readers have responded

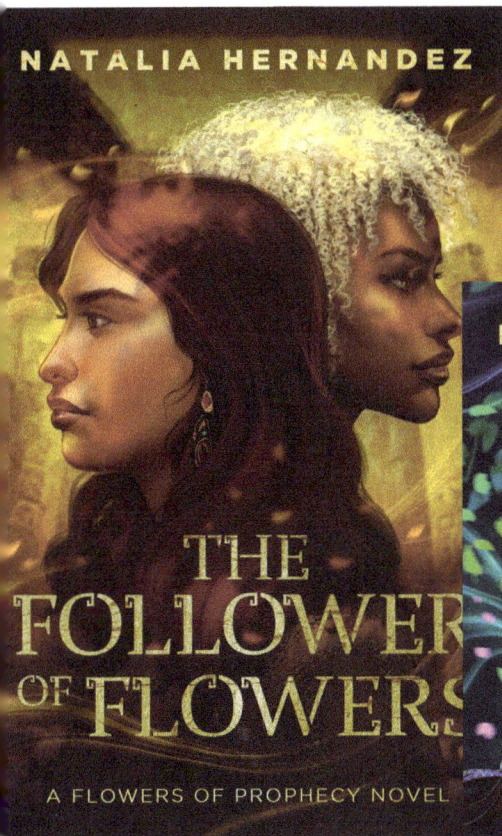

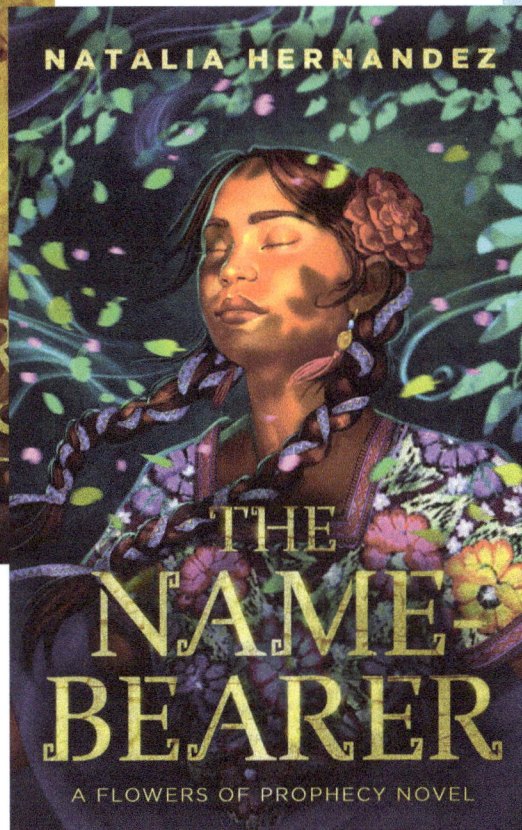

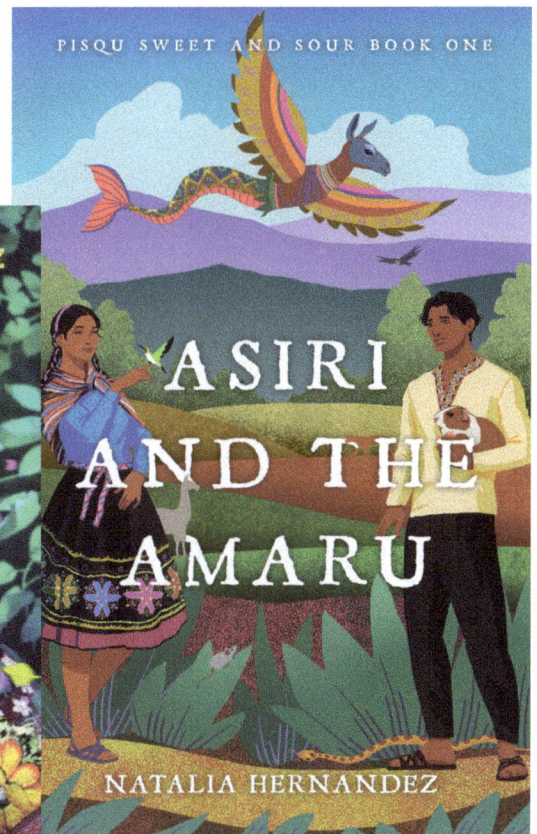

enthusiastically. "I get comments saying, 'Oh, my gosh! I've never seen anyone look like me on the cover of a book before!'" she says. Despite the reticence of the agents she queried, Natalia believes representation in media benefits both the readers who feel seen and those who may not have had exposure to characters who don't look like them. "The more you are seen in media, the more accepted you are, and the less division there is in the world," she says.

In her next book, an unconnected adult Cozy Fantasy titled *Asiri and the Amaru*, she incorporated more of her family's Peruvian folklore, and the cultural details she noticed in Guatemala, from food and clothing to language. "Latin people are not a monolith, you know. There's so many different countries, and dialects, and slang, and food. So I just took a little bit of all of it—anything that I knew well," she says.

She started seeking out and reading other Fantasy novels based in Latin American cultures, setting up an Amazon wishlist to share her new finds with followers. When she told them what she wanted to do—learn more about fantasy and mythology of other cultures—readers purchased books from her list and sent them to her. The support was unexpected, but it confirmed the potential of her social media presence to grow her business.

BUILDING A SUSTAINABLE CAREER

When it came time to purchase services like editing and cover design, Natalia had set some money aside from her marketing job, but she needed help to reach her goals. She set up a GoFundMe instead of a Kickstarter because the expectations of the tiers made her nervous. Fighting impostor syndrome and anxiety around finishing the book and publishing it herself, she decided to put it in the hands of her followers. "So I just said, if people want to support me, that would be amazing, but that will be out of the goodness of their heart. Whatever was raised would be so appreciated," she says.

They raised over $5,000.

As a first-time, as-yet-unpublished indie author, Natalia was overwhelmed by the support. She continued to post TikToks with updates on her progress, using trending audios to share snippets of character interactions, and her followers came along for the ride. Within four months of launching her debut novel, she knew she could afford to quit her day job. Six months after releasing *The Name-Bearer,* she did, without ever having paid for ads.

It was a leap of faith, but she promised herself that if she couldn't make her business sustainable in a year, she would get another job. Having another career to fall back on gave her the courage to put all her efforts into publishing and marketing her books. "But I worked very, very hard that year to make sure that I didn't go back and get another real job," she says, smiling.

She started by setting up a website with WooCommerce, but most of her direct sales still go through TikTok. When asked if she has advice for other new authors starting in direct sales, she laughs. It's a moment of disbelief in her own accomplishment that belies her easy confidence. "I never expected that it would be the grand portion of my author career, or how I'm able to continue doing what I'm doing. I'm so grateful that I continue to get so many direct sales."

Lately, she's been spending her mornings packing and shipping fifty to two hundred orders a day. She says staying on top of inventory is probably the most important thing "because the worst thing that you can do is sell more than you have in stock, or have a video go viral and you don't have enough boxes or shippers to send them out in. It can get very overwhelming very quickly. So organization is key."

She's started looking for a virtual assistant to help organize some of the business routines that have fallen to the side, like her newsletter and Patreon accounts. In the meantime, once she's finished packing orders for the day, she spends the afternoon nurturing her TikTok followers and her evenings writing in sprints with partners like Isabelle Olmo, author of The Queen's Red Guard series.

Natalia says, "The community is one of the best parts of this entire author journey." Although she is an extrovert, she doesn't get lonely working from home because she finds her online interactions with readers, writers, and BookTokers as fulfilling as if they were in person. "It feels like constant companionship," she says.

Although her definition of success continues to evolve with her career, one thing is certain: she's not going back. "This is what I want to do," she says. "I've never felt happier or more fulfilled in my professional career than right now, and I loved all my jobs."

Looking back on her first year as a full-time author, she sees her new business as the culmination of everything that's come before, from her childhood stories to her work as a freelance makeup artist to her product marketing job. "It all just sort of came together to support [my author career], and I think that was really interesting. You never know what path your life is going to take you, but I don't think anything that you've done before doesn't serve a purpose," she says. ∎

Jenn Lessmann

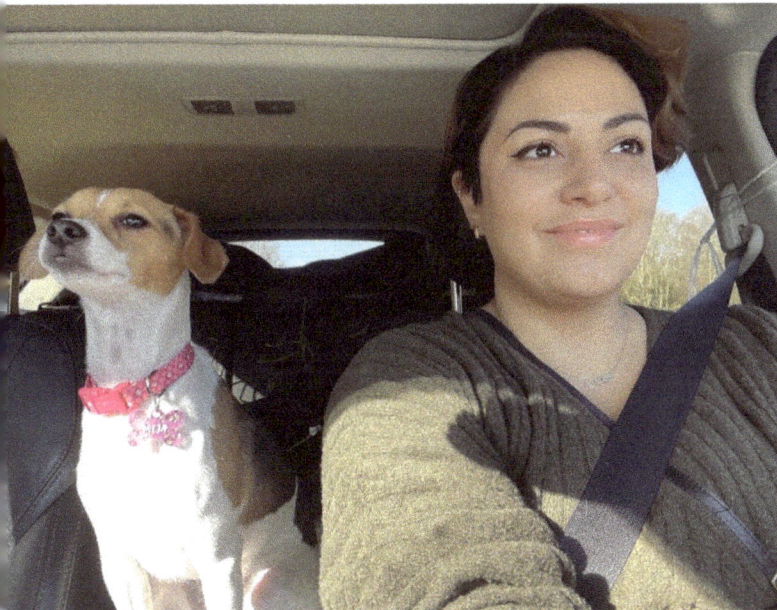

Jenn Lessmann

Jenn Lessmann is the author of Unmagical: a Witchy Mystery and three stories on Kindle Vella. A former barista, stage manager, and high school English teacher with advanced degrees from impressive colleges, she continues to drink excessive amounts of caffeine, stay up later than is absolutely necessary, and read three or four books at a time. Jenn is currently studying witchcraft and the craft of writing, and giggling internally whenever they intersect. She writes snarky paranormal fantasy for new adults whenever her dog will allow it.

Nature or Nurture?

USING BOTH ORGANIC AND PAID TRAFFIC TO BUILD A SUSTAINABLE BOOK BUSINESS

Under the umbrella of traffic, you can attract a potential reader's attention in two ways: naturally, through your interactions with readers online, through social media, or in person; or by nurturing a new connection with paid advertising and marketing opportunities. When you spend money to hopefully purchase a specific audience's attention, you're engaging in advertising. Organic traffic is the opposite, using no money at all for a reader's attention.

When discussing marketing and promotion strategies, authors often treat organic traffic and paid traffic as entirely different categories. But both means of gathering readers' attention offer valuable tools for an author's tool chest. Although they are different in execution, the data each provides can help you bolster the other, growing your business in every direction.

TARGET AUDIENCES

In an ideal scenario, your readers, whether brought to your books by organic or paid marketing methods, will be of the same audience. That audience should be your ideal reader: the person most likely to purchase and enjoy your book. The first step to analyzing your traffic is to consider what your readers expect from the books they enjoy, and how your work fulfills those expectations.

Across the internet, readers' attention is divided. There are hundreds of apps, services, and companies attempting to capture their customers' attention. Readers have become desensitized to the noise, which leaves authors looking to grow their traffic an opportunity to stand out by speaking directly to a reader and making them feel heard. View your conversations with readers as an opportunity to notice them rather than notify them. There is an unspoken association with how much effort an author gives to connecting with their readers and how much the reader then feels compelled to give that author their attention. Authors can tap into this connection in paid and unpaid advertising if they are willing to speak to their readers how they are best spoken to.

Some of the best performing pay-per-click ads started off as social media posts, such as TikTok or Instagram Reels. Your organic content, especially that content which performs best in terms of engagement, reach, or clicks, is ripe and tested ad copy for your paid ads, and it works because you've already seen proof that it connects with your target audience. Readers want to be noticed, and when they engage with your organic content, that is a sign that your audience has felt compelled enough to interact with whatever you have posted.

Equally, paid traffic should not be neglected as a source of information about your readers. If an ad is converting particularly well, analyze that ad to determine what about it is working. Does the copy address something your readers have been talking about or asking for? Are you solving a problem for them? Do you have a compelling offer? Is the imagery or video scroll-stopping? If your ad is only converting while your book is discounted, it may be your offer that's attracting potential readers to click. However, if the book is full priced and has consistent sales, your ad copy, landing page, and description may be connecting with your readers.

With both strategies, consider where your ideal audience likes to hang out. Your target audience likely has a preferred social media app or digital space. Whether that be TikTok, Facebook, Instagram, X, or somewhere else, you should attempt to create content that not only speaks to your ideal reader but also reaches them where they have a higher likelihood of finding it. Just like with paid traffic, pushing the wrong kind of organic traffic, or pushing organic traffic to the wrong place, will yield less optimal results than if you meet your customer where they hang out and speak to them in a way they prefer.

KEY PERFORMANCE INDICATORS

Any paid advertising will be loaded with Key Performance Indicators (KPIs) that can help you formulate strategies for your website and social media presences, drawing the attention of your organic audience as well. Examples of KPIs are clicks, conversions to sales, and click-through-rates, and depending on your sales strategies, each one has a different value for your business. For example, authors using direct sales are most likely to find value out of and accurately track conversions of an ad thanks to the analytics on the back end of their storefront. An author focusing on sending traffic to retailers, on the other hand, might look at engagement and cost-per-click metrics to critique their ad's performance. In all this examination, you're looking for metrics that signal a perfect combination of copy and content that readers have no choice but to engage with, and identifying the crossroads between where your reader feels noticed most and your content.

Organic traffic refers to the audience you attract through unpaid avenues, but that doesn't mean the content you create for these readers isn't targeted. Just like with paid ad KPIs, when discussing the performance of organic traffic, there are KPIs an author can use to determine the quality of their organic advertising efforts.

Core social media KPIs include engagement, follower metrics, and conversion click-through rate. These are performance indicators outside the sale itself, and while actual sales numbers are important, you should analyze the data provided by your marketing campaigns to diagnose what is working and what isn't. These metrics are found on the back end of social media channels and email service providers, and most offer breakdowns by KPI, date, age, and more useful identifiers to help you evaluate your audience.

Here's a more in-depth look at how to evaluate some common KPI metrics for the health of your connection with your audience.

Engagement

Engagement simply means how someone is interacting with your content. This can mean likes, comments, shares, and clicks. With engagement, the user has taken an action with the content, meaning you have captured their attention long enough to stop their scrolling. Look for posts that see more interaction overall to analyze what catches people's eyes the most, and consider what your audience or the algorithm prefers on each platform—your Facebook followers may enjoy longer text posts if they include images, and Instagram may prioritize Reels or carousel posts over single images.

Follower Metrics

Follower metrics reveal the rate at which you are gaining new followers, which reflects how well you're speaking to your target audience. If someone follows you, this is supposed to mean they want to see more of what you have to offer.

This doesn't account for a small but engaged following compared with a larger, unengaged audience. KPIs can reflect this concept. TikTok, for example, shows how well received videos are by your current following, and how many followers followed you from a specific video. TikTok also shows you how many of your current followers watched your videos. These metrics show the health of your following beyond sheer numbers and will help determine how engaging your content really is.

Conversion Click-Through Rate

At the end of a person's interaction with your content, your goal might be a purchase, at which point the click-through-rate (CTR)—the number of users who clicked a link you've directed them to within your content—can be examined. CTR means you've not just gotten the user's attention, but you've also compelled them enough to look at what you have to offer. Both paid and organic traffic can benefit from a look at CTR, but how to calculate the efficacy of your content will depend on the method you're using—organic traffic is most cost effective to test, for example, whereas paid traffic can offer the most predictable results.

Although organic and paid traffic have their distinct advantages, there is some crossover between both sides of the traffic coin that can give you valuable knowledge by which to judge how well you know your target audience. No matter your strategy, organic traffic is a good place to start determining what your paid content audience will best respond to, and your paid audience will show you what messages truly resonate with your target audience, even if they found you organically. Use the data to your advantage to make the most well-informed, well-considered decisions, and think like an entrepreneur, ready to use every tool available. ■

David Viergutz

David Viergutz

David Viergutz is a disabled Army Veteran, Law Enforcement Veteran, husband and proud father. He is an author of stories from every flavor of horror and dark fiction. One day, David's wife sat him down and gave him the confidence to start putting his imagination on paper. From then on out his creativity has no longer been stifled by self-doubt and he continues to write with a smile on his face in a dark, candle-lit room.

On Brand

SIX STEPS TO PERFECTING YOUR BUSINESS'S BRAND AND ATTRACTING THE RIGHT READERS

"Brand or be branded," says branding expert Deb Gabor, bestselling author of *Branding Is Sex*. Even if you don't have a personal brand, your readers are already branding you. The impression you leave—intentionally or not—will stick, and it will shape how your work is perceived and remembered.

For a self-published author, building a strong personal brand helps you to control that perception, stand out from the crowd, and build a lasting connection with your audience. Personal branding is the art of shaping and managing how you are perceived by others. For authors, it goes beyond promoting your books; it's about creating a compelling narrative around who you are as a writer. This involves your personality, values, expertise, and public image, which all come together to form your unique identity. A strong personal brand can help you gain credibility, attract loyal readers, and differentiate you from your peers.

KEY ELEMENTS OF PERSONAL BRANDING

The key elements of authenticity, consistency, value proposition, and engagement serve as the blueprint for aligning your business with your unique identity and values. From conveying your voice to building meaningful relationships with your audience, incorporating these elements into every interaction will strengthen your personal brand and set you apart.

Authenticity

Authenticity forms the foundation of a strong personal brand. To create a genuine connection with your audience, you need to stay true to yourself, conveying your unique voice, beliefs, and passions in every interaction. Authenticity doesn't just mean being honest; it also means allowing your personality to shine through in your communication.

Readers appreciate authors who are transparent about their journey, including the challenges and triumphs along the way. Whether you're sharing your writing process, talking about your inspirations, or discussing the themes in your books, it's essential to be sincere. This approach not only helps to build trust with your audience but also sets you apart in a world where authenticity can be rare. When your audience feels they know the real you, they're more likely to become invested in your work and support your career.

Pro Tip: Remember, you can still be authentic even if your brand is built around a pen name or a fictional character. The key is to be consistent with the voice and values your brand persona conveys.

Consistency

Consistency is the glue that holds your personal brand together, helping you build brand recognition and trust. To maintain a cohesive presence across platforms, you need to ensure your messaging, imagery, and overall style are aligned. This means using a consistent tone in your communications, having a recognizable visual identity, and keeping your branding elements uniform.

From your website and social media profiles to book covers and promotional materials, consistency creates a sense of reliability for readers. It also makes it easier for them to recognize your work at a glance, whether they're browsing online or attending a book event. Inconsistent branding can confuse your audience and weaken your brand's impact. By committing to a consistent approach, you reinforce your identity and make it easier for your audience to engage with and remember you.

Value Proposition

A clear value proposition acts as a North Star, serving as a unique and persuasive statement that communicates why readers should be interested in their work. For example, an author specializing in Psychological Thrillers may emphasize their ability to keep readers on the edge of their seats with unexpected twists and turns. Another author focusing on heartwarming Romance novels might highlight their talent for creating emotionally resonant love stories that leave readers feeling uplifted.

These examples of value propositions can be effectively integrated into an author's branding and advertising strategies. Authors can feature these unique selling points as a tagline on their websites, in their social media profiles, and alongside other marketing assets to attract the attention of the right readers. By consistently reinforcing these key elements of their value proposition across different marketing channels, authors can cultivate a strong and recognizable brand identity that resonates with their target audience, ultimately driving increased visibility and sales for their books.

Engagement

Personal branding isn't just about sending messages; it's about creating meaningful connections with your audience. Engagement is key to building these relationships, and it involves more than just sharing that you have a new book out. To truly engage with your audience, you need to create opportunities for interaction and dialogue, be it through social media, newsletters, blog posts, and events, where you can connect with readers on a personal level.

Responding to comments, answering questions, and asking for feedback are all effective ways to foster engagement. Additionally, hosting live sessions, Q&A events, or virtual book clubs can create a sense of community among your readers. By engaging with your audience in meaningful ways, you show that you value their input and are interested in building a lasting relationship. This not only strengthens your personal brand but also encourages readers to become advocates for your work, helping to spread the word and attract new fans.

PERSONAL BRANDING STRATEGIES

Creating a successful personal brand means crafting a unique identity that resonates with your audience. This involves developing a strategy for conveying your brand's message and purpose. The following six steps can help break down the process and make it easier to identify the building blocks that will ultimately define your brand in readers' eyes.

1. Define Your Author Persona
A clearly defined author persona offers continuity in your messaging and ensures your brand connects with your desired audience. Reflect on your values, interests, and writing style to create a cohesive and authentic brand identity. Consider what makes you unique as an author and what aspects of your personality you want to share with your audience. This persona will steer your marketing and branding choices going forward. For newer authors, it can take time to develop these guidelines, but for seasoned authors, it may simply be a matter of finding the aspects of your business that you've connected with the most or that you'd want your readers to highlight in reviews.

2. Develop a Compelling Author Bio
An author bio is like a snapshot of who you are and what you stand for. Creating an engaging author bio goes beyond just listing your background and achievements. It serves as a crucial element of your author brand, shaping how readers perceive you. For instance, a mystery writer's bio may incorporate elements that reflect the intrigue or suspense they weave into their stories. By infusing your bio with personality and aligning it with the themes of your work, you can reinforce your identity and leave a lasting impression on your readers. A memorable author bio can be a powerful tool for attracting readers and leaving a lasting impression, so take the time to craft it carefully.

    Pro Tip: Traditionally, author bios are written in the third person and should be concise and to the point, ranging from a few sentences to a short paragraph. However, don't be afraid to experiment with writing your bio in the first person if it better suits your brand and genre. This can help establish a more personal connection with your readers and showcase your individuality as an author.

3. Create Consistent Branding Elements

Authors can convey their brand's message and make their work more immediately identifiable through certain visual elements common across all platforms and materials, such as cohesive color schemes, typography, and imagery that align with their genre and brand identity.

Enlist the help of a designer or use online platforms that offer logo and color scheme creation services to ensure your branding aligns with your genre, style, personal aesthetic, and brand message or theme. This support can save you time and effort while allowing you to still present a polished and professional image to your audience.

4. Build a Strong Online Presence

In today's digital age, a solid online presence is crucial for personal branding. Start by establishing a professional website or landing page that showcases your books, author bio, blog posts, and upcoming events. This website should be easy to navigate and visually appealing, providing a hub for all things related to your writing. In addition to your website, either maintain an active profile on social media frequented by your target audience or find a communication channel that works for you, such as an online newsletter. Engage with followers by sharing content related to your writing niche and responding to comments and messages. A strong online presence not only helps you reach a wider audience but also allows you to build meaningful connections with readers. Plus, you'll be able to reiterate your brand and its message in each of your interactions.

5. Collaborate and Network

By teaming up with fellow authors in the same or similar genres, influencers who align with their brand, and industry experts, authors can broaden their audience reach through joint promotions, guest blog posts, interviews, and virtual events.

This collaborative approach not only increases visibility and therefore brand awareness, but it also lends credibility by associating you with other established figures in the field. Moreover, networking with industry professionals can provide valuable insights and opportunities for your continued growth, especially if they have an established relationship with your target audience.

6. Monitor and Adapt Your Strategy

Personal branding is not a one-time effort; it requires continuous refinement and adaptation. To keep your brand fresh and relevant, seek feedback from readers, peers, and mentors. This feedback can provide insights into how your brand is perceived and highlight areas for improvement. Use this information to adjust your branding strategy, whether that means refining your messaging, updating your visual elements, or changing your engagement approach. By continuously iterating on your personal brand, you can ensure that it remains effective and resonates with your target audience as much as possible, ultimately helping you build a stronger connection with your readers.

By incorporating these strategies into your marketing efforts, the possibilities for growth and success are limitless. It can take time to build a personal brand. But focusing on authenticity, consistency, and engagement will help you develop a brand that stands out, connects with readers, and ultimately creates a loyal fan base. ■

Angela Archer

Angela Archer

Having worked as a mental health nurse for many years, Angela combines her love of words with her love of human psychology to work as a copywriter in the UK. She independently published a novella and novel in 2020 and is currently fending off the lure of shiny new novel ideas to complete the second book in her sci-fi series. When she's not tinkering with words, she's usually drinking tea, playing the saxophone (badly), or being mum and wife to her husband and two boys.

Turning Lookie-Loos into Loyal Readers

WHAT IT TAKES TO COMPLETE THE TRANSMEDIA FUNNEL

The modern publishing landscape is a vast and dynamic arena, and authors are no longer confined to the traditional printed page. Today's storytellers are weaving intricate narratives that span multiple platforms, captivating audiences through a diverse array of mediums. This is the realm of transmedia storytelling, a powerful tool that can expand an author's reach, deepen fan engagement, and even generate additional income.

Unlike adaptations of books into different formats like e-books and audiobooks, transmedia encompasses a range of creative endeavors, from immersive video games and companion web series that delve into character backstories to podcasts that offer additional insights, augmented reality experiences, and merchandise.

"Transmedia storytelling allows you to extend your intellectual property while maintaining control over your narrative," says Fantasy and Sci-Fi author Jim Wilbourne. "By licensing your story world to other creators, such as filmmakers or game developers, you can attract new audiences who might then become interested in your books."

THE TRANSMEDIA FUNNEL: GOING WIDE AND GOING DEEP

Transmedia can be broadly categorized into two approaches: going wide and going deep.

Going wide involves creating new storytelling experiences across various platforms, potentially attracting a broader audience. "This could be a video game based on your dystopian world, where the game introduces players to the universe," Wilbourne says. "They might then decide to read the novel for a deeper experience."

Going deep, on the other hand, focuses on deepening relationships with existing fans. This might involve creating supplementary content like character profiles, maps, timelines, short stories, or audio dramas that expand on minor characters or events. The American sitcom *The Office* sparked several successful examples of this method, creating email exchanges and video shorts not aired on TV that enriched the viewer's experience and expanded on character relationships developed in the show.

THE CHALLENGE: CONVERTING AUDIENCES INTO READERS

Transmedia offers exciting opportunities, but it also presents a challenge: converting those who engage with your story through other mediums into readers of your books. It's possible to attract fans who are passionate about your world but never pick up your novels, so connecting the dots that bring a passive audience into your book business can be more important—and require more work—than meets the eye.

Chrishaun Keller, an author who has navigated the transmedia landscape, emphasizes the importance of making each piece of content feel essential. "Your fans should feel like they're getting a fuller experience by engaging with all parts of your story world," she says.

So how can authors bridge the gap between transmedia fans and book readers?

Integrated Storytelling: Ensure that each piece of transmedia content is woven into the fabric of the overall story, offering a deeper understanding of the world and characters. For instance, a video game might unlock additional chapters in a novel upon completion, or a podcast might offer clues that enhance the reading experience.

Cross-Promotion: Utilize each platform to promote the others, subtly guiding fans toward your books. Include book excerpts in web series or comics, mention your novels in podcasts, and use social media to connect different pieces of content. A well-placed QR code in a comic book or a link in a podcast description can seamlessly lead fans to your books.

Exclusive Content: Offer exclusive content or early access to fans who engage with multiple platforms, incentivizing them to explore your books. This could be in the form of bonus chapters, behind-the-scenes peeks, or even early access to new releases.

Community Building: Foster a vibrant community around your story world, encouraging fans to connect with one another and share their enthusiasm for your work. Host online Q&As, live readings, or virtual book clubs to create a sense of belonging and deepen their connection to your stories. As people talk about your story world and the ways they've interacted with it, they'll be able to provide a road map for new fans who are just starting to explore your content.

Gamification: Incorporate gamification elements into your transmedia strategy. Create challenges, quizzes, or scavenger hunts that reward fans for engaging with different platforms, ultimately leading them to your books.

MONETIZING YOUR TRANSMEDIA EFFORTS

Transmedia isn't just about fan engagement; it can also be a lucrative endeavor. Complete your funnel, and these alternate storytelling mediums may help supplement your business's income between books while also increasing readership and generating excitement for future releases.

Consider the following methods for growing your business financially via transmedia content.

Crowdfunding: Platforms like Kickstarter and Indiegogo can be powerful tools for funding transmedia projects and engaging your audience. Offer exclusive rewards like signed copies, character art, or a chance to be written into the next story.

Licensing: Partnering with other creators and companies to develop transmedia content can be a significant source of revenue. Licensing your story world for adaptations into comics, games, or films can open up new markets and attract a wider audience.

Merchandise: Develop merchandise related to your story world, such as T-shirts, mugs, or replica props. This not only generates income but also allows fans to express their love for your work.

Premium Content: Offer premium content like extended cuts of web series, ad-free podcasts, or early access to new releases for a fee. Consider creating a subscription service that gives members exclusive access to a variety of transmedia content.

THE FUTURE OF TRANSMEDIA

As technology continues to evolve, the possibilities for transmedia storytelling are limitless. Virtual reality, augmented reality, and interactive narratives are just a few of the emerging mediums that authors can explore to create even more immersive and engaging experiences for their fans. The rise of generative AI is poised to further revolutionize the landscape, offering authors unprecedented tools for expanding their reach and diversifying their content.

The key is to embrace experimentation, stay attuned to your audience's preferences, and always prioritize the core of your story. By doing so, you can not only expand your reach and deepen engagement but also forge a lasting connection with your readers, turning them into lifelong fans. The transmedia landscape is constantly evolving, and authors who are willing to embrace innovation and think outside the box could be well positioned for success in the years to come. Whether you're a seasoned pro or just starting out, the possibilities are endless. So dive in, experiment, and let your imagination run wild. Your story is waiting to be told—across a multitude of platforms. ∎

Chelle Honiker

Chelle Honiker

Chelle Honiker is an advocate for the empowerment of authorpreneurs, recognizing the importance of authors taking charge of both their craft and careers. In response to this need, she has founded a media and training company dedicated to supporting these creative professionals. With a career spanning over two decades in executive operations and leadership, Chelle has honed her skills in managing complex projects and delivering impactful training programs. Her experience as a speaker and TEDx Organizer has taken her to many countries, where she has shared her insights with diverse audiences.

A 'Book Cave' of Wonders

SIX MARKETING FEATURES THAT MAKE THE MARKETING SERVICE WORTH EXPLORING

As an indie publisher, you have likely built up a hoard of shiny, eye-catching ideas about how to get the word out about your books over the course of your author journey. Unfortunately, the sheer number of opportunities may be enough to paralyze your inner marketing dragon.

If you are looking for convenient ways to promote your books or expand your marketing strategy to a wider selection of readers, Book Cave's unique mix of features could simplify your life. The marketing service offers digital book delivery for free books, paid newsletter promotions, author group promotions, and movie-like content ratings for books, and it boasts a community of readers already using the site. Many services on the platform are free, so you're able to spend your treasure on other things; the cost for other services is based on your book's genre and price.

This month, we're exploring six of Book Cave's most enticing features. Read on to decide whether one of these marketing routes sounds right for your business.

1. A COMMUNITY-MANAGED MOVIE-LIKE RATING SYSTEM

Unique to Book Cave is a content ratings system for books, modeled on the movie industry and determined by Book Cave's own community of readers. My Book Ratings (MBR) is like Goodreads or LibraryThing in that readers can submit their own ratings for titles. As an author, target your book's audience more clearly by filling out the MBR questionnaire for each of your titles. You also have the option of paying Book Cave for an official rating. Publishers and authors who share the MBR logo and book rating on other sites are required to submit a listing to the Community Book Ratings database.

The Community Book Rating questionnaire creates a "free, permanent book listing that many readers use to find books in their comfort

level," according to the site. When authors book a newsletter promotion, the book listing will also appear on Book Cave's "Deals From Retailers" page: https://mybookcave.com/books. New readers are drawn to Book Cave's site through its book deal newsletter, e-reader and tablet giveaways, and book rating database.

Price: Community Book Ratings, which display an average rating between an author's self-report and readers who have rated, are free. Official Book Cave Ratings cost between $25 and $75, depending on book length.

2. SUBSCRIBER MAGNET DELIVERY

Along with sharing content reviews and information about your books, Book Cave also offers some distribution opportunities. Users can create unique links for their marketing, deliver advance review copies, or reward email subscribers with a freebie or a sample of their work.

Book Cave integrates with AWeber, Mailchimp, MailerLite, ConvertKit, EmailOctopus, Mad Mimi, SendFox, and Zagomail, so readers who download books through Book Cave are automatically added to authors' mailing lists. The dropdown menu lets you choose from your email lists, or groups, for each subscriber magnet. Book Cave only supports EPUB and MOBI formats. Each subscriber magnet can have multiple unique links, so it's easy to track the number of downloads from each newsletter swap, group promotion, or push for reviews. You can also limit the total number of downloads per link, make links active, or turn them off completely.

Pro Tip: Book Cave's blog has a step-by-step tutorial with screenshots to guide you through the process of uploading your subscriber magnet, as well as other useful tips and strategies for authors. Visit https://mybookcave.com/authorposts, then select "Tutorials" on the right side or search for a specific topic.

Some email services aren't supported, and Book Cave doesn't have an API or the ability to connect to Zapier to create a workaround. Book Cave doesn't support direct sales or audiobooks; the site refers authors to BookFunnel for that.

Price: Free

3. GROUP AUTHOR PROMOTION FOR MAGNETS

Like other book promotion sites, Book Cave offers users the ability to organize group promotions with other authors in order to build email lists and boost reach for everyone involved. As promo organizer, you can choose to add a giveaway prizes for up to ten winners, as well as choose which authors' email lists will receive entrants' sign-up information. Possible prizes for readers include $10 to $100 gift cards for Amazon, Barnes & Noble, or Apple Books; or a Kindle or Nook device.

Discover existing group promotions in Book Cave's Facebook group, in the site's author newsletter, or on the author dashboard, where you can also apply to participate in group promotions. You can also create your own group promotion with step-by-step tools. Email Book Cave about your group promotion to feature your group promotion on its author-facing pages and in its author newsletter. You also have the option to limit your promotion to a private group of authors.

Price: Free, but authors can add an optional paid giveaway; Book Cave fees are based on a book's genre and retail price.

4. FEATURE YOUR BOOK OR SERIES

Book Cave's newsletter will advertise your free or discounted book or series to its subscribers and on its website for a fee. The company estimates its total subscribers at 117,000 and its total social media reach at 225,000 followers. Book Cave supports thirty-six genres and subgenres, and its MBRs offer additional information about themes and topics that may help match books more closely with readers. Subscribers to Book Cave's newsletter fill out their preferences about genre, ratings, and themes, includes trigger warnings, when they sign up. Your book or series information will be saved, making repeat features convenient.

Pro Tip: Book Cave's minimum book length for promotion through the site is one hundred seventy pages. Formatting and grammatical errors can disqualify books, and ninety days must elapse between paid promotions. No serials are allowed, and digital box sets must be written by the same author.

Price: Paid, based on book genre and e-book price category (free, priced under $1, $1 to $1.99, and priced over $1.99). Series promotion ranges from $26 to $74, depending on genre and e-book price category. See https://bcd.mybookcave.com/subscribers-and-pricing for a complete pricing table and the number of subscribers for each genre.

5. AUTHOR PROFILE PAGE

Author profile pages offer another place to showcase your subscriber magnet, build your email list, notify book browsers about current paid Book Cave promotions, share your bio and a short interview, and share New Release Alerts with followers. Readers browsing retailer deals at https://mybookcave.com/books or the MBR database can connect to your email list through your subscriber magnet on the "Offers" tab.

Once you've created an author profile, followers will receive new release notifications and be notified by email whenever your books are

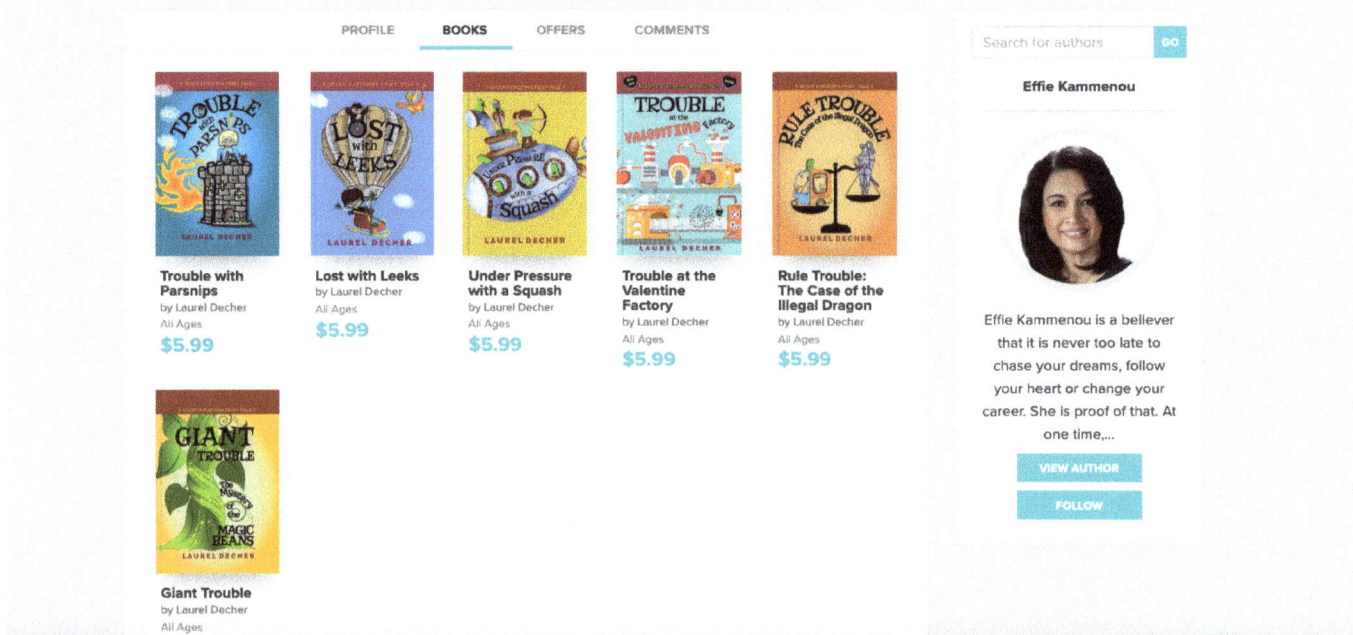

included in a Book Cave paid promotion. To get the "Offers" tab on your author profile, you must create a magnet and set it to public or be currently promoting a book or series with Book Cave. This feature is also the only place on the Book Cave site that allows a preorder promotion. The link to your author profile is shareable.

Price: Free

6. PRIVATE AND PUBLIC AUTHOR GROUP RETAILER PROMOTION

Authors can create their own group retailer promotions and recruit other authors by invitation only or with the help of Book Cave's author newsletter and author dashboard.

The group promotion organizer can screen participants to match the target audience. Authors can add a giveaway for readers for an additional fee.

Book Cave must create and manage group retailer promotions because of submission requirements and in order to issue invoices to participating authors. The site requires a minimum of thirty to thirty-five authors to cover advertising costs and the cost of the prize, if offered. Contact Book Cave for more information.

Price: $30 per participating author, which covers prizes and advertising.

With a flexible interface and the ability to connect with other authors and new readers, Book Cave is a unique platform that combines the best features of other popular book review and promotion sites into one. If your dragon's hoard of marketing strategies is feeling a bit thin, it may just be a treasure trove worth exploring. ■

Laurel Decher

Laurel Decher

There might be no frigate like a book, but publishing can feel like a voyage on the H.M.S. Surprise. There's always a twist and there's never a moment to lose. Laurel's mission is to help you make the most of today's opportunities. She's a strategic problem-solver, tool collector, and co-inventor of the "you never know" theory of publishing. As an epidemiologist, she studied factors that help babies and toddlers thrive. Now she writes books for children ages nine to twelve about finding more magic in life. She's a member of the Society for Children's Book Writers and Illustrators (SCBWI), has various advanced degrees, and a tendency to smuggle vegetables into storylines.

Modern Tales

THE DIFFERENCES BETWEEN CONTEMPORARY FICTION, CONTEMPORARY ROMANCE, AND LITERARY FICTION

Romance is, without a doubt, the largest genre with the most voracious readers, and according to a K-lytics report from 2024, it has seen nearly a 100 percent growth in the number of searches it receives on Google even in the last five years. The genre is categorized into well-defined subgenres that come with plenty of expectations from readers—and that includes Contemporary Romance, an expansive, thriving subgenre categorized by the time period of post–World War II to the present day.

Contemporary books find mass appeal in their relatability, and that isn't relegated to Romance alone. Other genres have adopted the umbrella term "contemporary" based on guidelines established in the book ecosystem of readers, authors, marketers, and writers. Contemporary stories, romances or otherwise, all contain modern themes and settings for maximum relatability with readers. So what sets them apart?

CONTEMPORARY ROMANCE

Contemporary Romance focuses on escapism through realism, drawing on modern social issues, societal shifts, and modern relationships. There is a heavy focus on the present, or near present, as characters live normal lives, and the reader is brought into that world. Readers should expect these stories to directly reflect their own experiences and emotions, allowing them to enjoy and connect with the characters more deeply. There are a few easy signals any writer in the genre can send to the reader that your story is exactly what readers are looking for.

Look for tropes such as the following to show up as building blocks in several popular Contemporary Romance stories:

Second Chances: In this trope, the relationship between characters has dissolved at some point, and new circumstances in life are giving the relationship another chance to thrive. Where the tension comes in is how the characters' lives have changed during the period of separation and how they must overcome those issues. Contemporary Romance, like all Romance, should ideally work toward a "happy for now" or "happily ever after" ending, according to Book Riot, depending on the author's plans for those characters in the future.

Enemies to Lovers: A trope with a huge payoff for the reader, "enemies to lovers" sets a character at odds with another character, making it seem as if they could never possibly get along, let alone be together. Characters start off opposing each other, and through their journey, they come to build a relationship and eventually fall in love, becoming allies rather than enemies.

Forbidden Love: A familiar trope famously seen in *Romeo and Juliet*, "forbidden love" pits a relationship against outside forces that are determined to keep the lovers apart. Strain on the characters' relationship doesn't come from within but from the outside world.

Of course, there are plenty more Romance tropes that can apply in contemporary stories as well as in any other subgenre. Find lists such as *Writer's Digest*'s "21 Popular Romance Tropes for Writers" for more ideas.

CONTEMPORARY FICTION

Outside of the tropes that make Contemporary Romance unique, there is a broader genre of Contemporary Fiction that embodies the same time frame without meeting the classifications of the Romance genre. Contemporary Fiction is a little less refined, defined largely by taking place in the present or recent past and allowing for the story to delve into more modern social, political, and cultural events. The genre finds success in its ability to connect with readers on topics they understand and find interest in. And while it may seem Contemporary Fiction is dominated by Romance, there is room for other genres to find a home under the umbrella term.

Science Fiction set in the present with real, modern science rather than speculation can hold the banner of Contemporary Fiction. Books like *Outbreak* by Robin Cook, published in 1987, might be considered both a Thriller and a Sci-Fi novel based on its heavy exploration of viral outbreaks of Ebola. Military Thrillers can also do the same if they draw from present events, even if the fiction is heavier with characters who are sometimes borderline action hero stars.

In Contemporary Fiction, there are a few opportunities to subvert reader expectations, but they generally lie on the fiction side of Contemporary Fiction.

LITERARY FICTION

When exploring Contemporary Fiction, it is important to distinguish between Contemporary Fiction and Literary Fiction. While Contemporary Fiction focuses on current events, societal issues, and modernism, Literary Fiction focuses on language and style in lieu of plot and character development. Nonetheless, Contemporary Fiction can be considered a subgenre of Literary Fiction. Further down the line, such as in the Military Thrillers mentioned before, elements such as mystery and thrills define further subgenres.

Contemporary Fiction should reflect the reader's world. A book's themes and topics explored within the story do best when the reader cares about the topics at hand, whether they be relationships, questions about scientific advancements, thrilling military adventures, or a deep exploration of human relationships. And while there is much overlap between Contemporary Fiction, Contemporary Romance, and Literary Fiction, a writer can do well by understanding what the reader expects from a given genre or subgenre—in this case, a story that seeks to comment on real-world situations rather than escape from them. ∎

David Viergutz

David Viergutz

David Viergutz is a disabled Army Veteran, Law Enforcement Veteran, husband and proud father. He is an author of stories from every flavor of horror and dark fiction. One day, David's wife sat him down and gave him the confidence to start putting his imagination on paper. From then on out his creativity has no longer been stifled by self-doubt and he continues to write with a smile on his face in a dark, candle-lit room.

Your Publisher Persona

A DIFFERENT WAY FOR INDIE AUTHORS TO APPROACH PUBLISHER EVENTS

Although many international book fairs, such as Bologna, London, or Frankfurt book fairs, have introduced author tracks or highlighted best-selling authors for prestigious readings in recent years, the primary players at these fairs are, and have been from the beginning, publishers. Conferences targeted at authors focus on the development of individual books or series, but a publishing fair is a marketplace for buying and selling intellectual property rights, and a place to showcase and debate new ideas about our industry.

As an indie author, you play the role of "publisher" as much as you do "author"; you know who your books are for, the needs your publishing satisfies, and the selling points that have already worked for each book or series. A book fair is the place to spell out your baked-in marketing hooks like holidays, current events, evergreen themes, curriculum tie-ins, or catchy book club discussion topics—and you'll do that most effectively when you're thinking like a publisher first.

THE FAIREST BOOKS OF ALL

When you prepare an artist's statement, a media or speaker's kit, a rights catalog, an events or news webpage, or a press release, you are spelling out your best ideas about how others can connect to your work. These are similar tools, but each is tailored to a different audience. These are exercises in strengthening your publishing point of view—highlighting how you, or others in the industry, can best understand and market your work. Where writing is a creative endeavor, publishing is a business, and that's the mindset you should take to these events.

With your publishing vision in mind, ahead of any book fair or publishing event, review the program, considering both presenters and vendors who will be attending. Create the marketing materials that appeal to you, and gather your messaging and promotional ideas together to make them shareable with others attending your event. Start pitching for appointments with professionals you'd like to meet at least twelve weeks ahead of time to allow for follow-up. Even if you aren't ready to discuss rights licensing, a conversation with an existing distributor or retailer might show your books in a new light and win them more visibility. A supplier or software developer might answer questions or offer answers that inspire a new publishing project with your existing books. An organization for foreign language editors might help with your translation needs. Author organizations may also be present at the fair to offer support in other areas of your business.

STUDYING PUBLISHERS IS FAIR PLAY

As both the creators and the sellers within their publishing businesses, book fairs are the perfect place for self-published authors to broaden their focus and imagine their future. Indie authors are often advised to study Amazon's categories to find where their books fit in the book market and understand what readers want. Visiting a book fair brings this to life as a maze of publishers, services, and organizations. Browse through the stands and take in the shapes, colors, formats, and mission statements of all the publishers. Who shares your aesthetic, purpose, or readers? Concrete examples will help you expand your publishing imagination.

Instead of comparative titles for your books, look for comparative publishers. Are there color palettes that clash or harmonize with your book covers? Do you see intriguing formats or themes that resonate with your work? Maybe you can gain gradual awareness of a new trend, like coloring books for adults. These insights can be tie-ins for your current publishing strategy or magic beans for the future.

The fair is also the perfect place to practice your talking and selling points and discover new ones. Bring copies of sell sheets and a printed catalog of your titles, so others can visualize your work at a glance and see where it might fit with their goals and so you can find potential collaborators to make your vision a reality.

THE RIGHTS GAME AND FAIR TRADES

Another benefit to attending publisher-focused events: more so than at author events, you'll likely be able to meet with those who could eventually license translation, film, or other rights to your work. The Alliance of Independent Authors' guide *How Authors Sell Publishing Rights* describes what rights author-publishers have, details the role of agents and lawyers in the process, and gives practical tips about how to prepare for book fairs, make pitches, and understand contracts.

As always, a crucial and intangible benefit to braving the woods is the sheer energy of the book fair. Just the knowledge that thousands of people think books are vital to our lives can encourage and inspire a flagging and weary indie publisher. Books are worthy of the dedicated—and sometimes exhausting—work necessary to bring them to readers. Your work in publishing has brought you to a new gateway. What conversations would you like to take part in? What movements would you like to support? Who do you want to entertain? An international book fair is a place for discourse about ideas that affect our world, and you're a publisher who deserves to be part of it. ■

Laurel Decher

Laurel Decher

There might be no frigate like a book, but publishing can feel like a voyage on the H.M.S. Surprise. There's always a twist and there's never a moment to lose. Laurel's mission is to help you make the most of today's opportunities. She's a strategic problem-solver, tool collector, and co-inventor of the "you never know" theory of publishing. As an epidemiologist, she studied factors that help babies and toddlers thrive. Now she writes books for children ages nine to twelve about finding more magic in life. She's a member of the Society for Children's Book Writers and Illustrators (SCBWI), has various advanced degrees, and a tendency to smuggle vegetables into storylines.

CLONE YOURSELF

Custom Chat GPT Bots

Harnessing AI's knowledge base and expand your skills and expertise in vital areas such as:

Life and Business Coaching
Mastering Marketing and Newsletter Strategies
Crafting Captivating Blurbs and Social Posts
Enhancing Time Management
Elevating Customer Service
Writing Compelling Ad, Product, and Landing Page Copy

And that's just the beginning.

INDIEAUTHORTRAINING.COM

INDIE AUTHOR MAGAZINE

HELLO AND WELCOME!

I'm Indie Annie, and I'm thrilled you're reading this gorgeous full-color version of IAM. Did you know that you can also access all the information, education, and inspiration in our app? It's available on both the iOS App Store and Google Play. And for those that prefer to listen to me read articles, you can pop over to Spotify or our website.
Happy Reading!

IndieAuthorMagazine.com

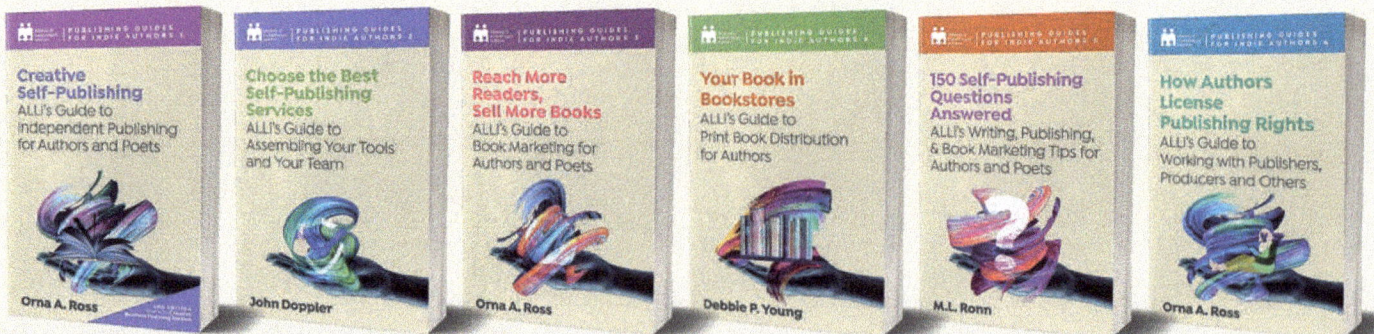